Over 120 delicious recipes:

Barbecue

Over 120 delicious recipes:

Barbecue

Elisabeth Lang

**DUMONT
monte**

Beef: Buy high-quality beef from a butcher you can trust. Ask about its origin and that it was properly slaughtered in compliance with the regulations.

Eggs: If not otherwise stated, the eggs used in these recipes are of medium size.

Milk: If not otherwise stated, milk used in these recipes is whole milk (3.5% fat content).

Poultry: Poultry should always be cooked right through before eating. You can tell if it is done by piercing it with a skewer. If the juices run out pink, then it is not ready and must be cooked for a longer time. If the juices are clear then the bird is done.

Nuts: Some of these recipes contain nuts or nut oil. People who have allergies or who tend to be allergic should avoid eating these dishes.

Herbs: If not otherwise stated, these recipes call for fresh herbs. If you cannot obtain these, the amounts in the recipes can be replaced with half the quantity of dried herbs.

Olive oil: The taste of olive oil varies considerably. It is a good idea to have two olive oils available. The best extra-virgin olive oil is suitable for making salads, raw vegetables, steamed vegetable and pasta dishes. It can be heated up to 350°F (180°C). For roasting and grilling on the barbecue ordinary olive oil is better since it can be heated up to 410°F (210°C). Cold-pressed olive oil is not suitable for grilling since it burns too easily. Olive oil should be stored at in a cool place (not in the refrigerator) away from the light.

Contents

Introduction

Barbecuing has an ancient history in many parts of the world, and since the 1950s has become increasingly popular in areas where the tradition is much more recent or even non-existent. It has become an engrossing hobby for many people. This is hardly surprising, because there is nothing pleasanter than being with a companionable gathering of friends and acquaintances round the barbecue, enjoying the delicious smells and atmosphere that accompany the barbecuing process – not to mention the culinary delights that it provides.

It is no longer simply skewered meat kebabs that sizzle above the embers. As well as making delicious, healthy side dishes, grilled vegetables can form mouthwatering main courses that appeal to gourmets in general and the many vegetarian barbecue enthusiasts in particular.

Barbecue equipment

As barbecuing has became progressively more popular in recent years, the industry has also grown more inventive. As a result there is now a wide variety of different types of barbecues and utensils.

Whether the barbecue grill uses charcoal, gas or electricity as a fuel, the flavor and aroma of the food prepared will not differ very much. The choice between one type of grill and another is therefore mainly a matter of convenience and personal taste. But there are differences in design and materials.

The most important aspect when choosing a barbecue is that it should stand firmly. The structure that supports it must be stable so that it will not collapse or fall over if accidentally knocked, which would be dangerous for people and/or the surroundings. Another aspect to consider when buying a barbecue is the quality. of construction and compliance with local safety standards. The height of the grid and spit above the heat should be adjustable. The height of the barbecue itself depends on where it will be used, as well as the owner's preference.

The classic barbecue grill

The charcoal barbecue is the commonest type. Its chief advantage is its mobility, enabling it to be used easily wherever it is permitted.

Both direct grilling and indirect barbecuing can be carried out on the charcoal barbecue. In the case of direct grilling, the charcoal is distributed evenly and the food is placed on a grid above it. For cooking large pieces such as joints of meat or a chicken, an electric spit is easier because it saves the need to turn the meat continuously by hand.

Strictly speaking, the term "barbecuing" specifically means cooking indirectly. In this case, the charcoal is stacked to one side and the grid is covered with a lid or cover so that the air heated by the charcoal surrounds the food evenly. A spit is not required with indirect heat. This method is used mainly for roasting larger pieces of meat.

Recently charcoal barbecuing has been the cause of some concern on account of possible health risks. When dripping fat burns on the open fire, benzopyrenes can be formed, and these carcinogenic substances may be absorbed by the food.

To prevent this from happening the food can be put on aluminum foil trays on top of the grid instead of directly on the grid itself. These trays are widely available. Some modern barbecues offer an alternative solution – the charcoal can simply be tossed to the side in a container to prevent fumes developing. The new types of bio-barbecues collect the dripping

fat along specially designed rods, transferring it to another container.

The fuel

Today charcoal is manufactured industrially from beech or other hardwood. With good quality charcoal all the pieces are the same size, and they should not be too small. Very small pieces are a sign of low quality; they burn much too quickly and are therefore unable to hold the heat. Cheap charcoal is also often polluted.

For large barbecues, charcoal briquettes are ideal. These are made of powdered charcoal that is pressed into briquettes. They take longer to reach the state where the charcoal is glowing right through, but as a result they hold the heat much longer than ordinary pieces of lump charcoal .

Slightly more expensive but environmentally friendly is charcoal made from coconut shells. This is a recent development that is popular because it burns for a long time and holds the heat well. The use of coconut shells is environmentally friendly because no trees have to be felled to provide them.

Tips for barbecuing with charcoal

- Watch out for the wind direction when setting up the barbecue so that the neighbors are not bothered by the smoke.
- The charcoal barbecue must be equipped with wind protection, preferably on three sides. This prevents the danger of hot ash and sparks being blown about. Position the wind protection so that it shelters the barbecue, letting the smoke rise straight up.

- The barbecue must stand firmly and securely on the ground, without wobbling.
- Never use liquid starters to light the charcoal. Use solid fire-lighters or wax or jelly starters.
- Paper or cardboard should never be used on a barbecue. The coloring agents and glues they contain could be damaging to health. Fir cones should not be used on barbecues either.

Lighting the charcoal

Line the fire bowl of the barbecue with foil and open the vents. To light the charcoal, use proprietary barbecue starters and place the cubes, crumbled pieces or jelly directly on the foil. Build a charcoal pyramid round and over the starter, then light with a match.

As soon as you see a few pieces of charcoal glowing, start fanning the fire with a pair of bellows or a folded newspaper. Then scatter the glowing charcoal or briquettes evenly over the fire bowl using a poker.

Let them burn until the flames have died down and the charcoal has formed a light gray layer of ash on its surface, under which a red glow can be seen.

This usually takes about 30 to 45 minutes. Do not start cooking until this stage is reached.

As a rule of thumb, the barbecue has reached the right temperature when you cannot hold your hand 6 in/15 cm above the fire for more than a couple of seconds. At this stage the vent should be closed a little or even completely. Oil the grid first so that the food will not stick. Then replace the grid above the embers so that the grid itself can heat up.

Adding more fuel to the barbecue

For a large barbecue party, the fire will have to last longer, remaining at a constant heat all the time. To achieve this, more charcoal or briquettes must be added. This should only be done when there is no food on the barbecue, otherwise charcoal dust or ash may be blown onto the food. One solution used by many barbecue experts is to divide the glowing charcoal into two smaller heaps. One heap is used for cooking the food while more charcoal is added to the other heap. When the second heap is glowing right through, it can be used for cooking the food.

Extinguishing the fire

The easiest way is to let the charcoal burn out completely. The vents should be closed while this takes place. If this is not possible, the fire can be extinguished by sprinkling sand on top. Never pour water over the charcoal – this will result in scalding steam and spluttering drops of dangerously hot water that could cause serious burns. When cold, the ashes should not be thrown away. They can be used in the garden as an excellent fertilizer for flowering plants, or added to the compost heap.

The permanent garden barbecue

A permanent barbecue is an ideal solution for people with a garden who often organize large barbecue parties. All that is needed for such a barbecue are a foundation, three walls made of bricks, building blocks or stone, and a grid placed across them. This can be home-built or a self-assembly kit can be used. The site is important. Because of the danger of fire, it should not be placed too close to the house. The direction of the wind is also a significant consideration in that the barbecue should be located where the smoke will not blow towards the house or your neighbors. You should also make sure that there is enough room round the barbecue for the guests to eat and enjoy themselves comfortably.

The gas barbecue

Gas barbecues make no smoke, so they are more "neighbor-friendly" than charcoal barbecues. They can be located quite close to the house, on a terrace, patio or deck.

Admittedly, a gas barbecue is not as mobile as a charcoal barbecue since it must always be connected to a gas tank. But a gas barbecue is extremely convenient for this very reason, since it does not need preheating. The grill develops its full heat more or less immediately after being lit. In addition, the temperature can be controlled by turning a knob. Where the radiant heat is transferred to the food from above, there is no risk of any health hazard from the burning of dripping fat.

Another type of gas barbecue uses lava stones. Lava stone is a porous material that radiates heat when heated from below by gas jets until it glows.

This creates an effect similar to that of a charcoal barbecue. Because the stone absorbs any dripping fat, no smoke with carcinogenic substances is produced.

Very practical: the electric barbecue

Electric barbecues can also be used inside the house so that barbecued dishes can be enjoyed at any time of the year, regardless of the weather or the season. They work on the same principle as gas barbecues: the lava stones are heated and produce a constant, even heat after a short warming-up period. Manufacturers have developed a wide range of electric barbecues, from the simple table barbecue to combination barbecues with microwave and conventional ovens.

Particularly popular: the table barbecue

Electric table barbecues that can be used in the garden, terrace, balcony or house are becoming increasingly popular. These portable barbecues are also very easy to clean because they can just be taken to pieces afterwards and washed in the dishwasher.

A word of warning: aluminum foil trays must not be used on electric barbecues. Always put the food directly on the grid or the barbecue may overheat.

Barbecue equipment

The range of accessories and barbecue equipment is even more impressive than the choice of barbecues. Some are very sensible and should be considered essentials:

- Barbecue gloves: Well-insulated gloves are invaluable when cooking on a barbecue. They protect your hands from splashes of hot fat as the food is turned. When buying these gloves, check that they are long enough to protect the wrist and if possible part of the forearm as well.

- Barbecue apron: The person cooking should always wear an apron made from strong fabric to protect the clothing and bare skin from splashes of hot fat. The apron must not contain any artificial fibers since these are highly flammable.
- Bellows: These are used to deliver the oxygen needed when lighting charcoal. Alternatively a folded newspaper cn be used to do the job.
- Poker: When cooking with charcoal, you need a poker to distribute the charcoal and glowing embers. The handle should be well insulated so that it does not become too hot from heat conducted up the metal.
- Barbecue tongs: Robust barbecue tongs make it easy to turn pieces of meat of any size. Do not use a fork to turn the meat because it will prick the meat and let the juices escape, so the meat may become dry.

- Hinged fish grilling basket: This wire basket makes it easy to turn the fish or other food over without it falling apart.
- Roasting rack: Useful for chickens and larger roasts, making them easier to manipulate.
- For carving meat: A carving fork, a large, sharp kitchen knife, and a chopping board with a groove all round to catch the juices.
- Strong aluminum foil should always be available when barbecuing. Very juicy vegetables such as tomatoes cannot be cooked very easily on a grid or skewer. They should be wrapped in aluminum and then cooked on the grid. Foil is also useful for lining the grid when cooking with charcoal. The shiny side should be face up and oiled well so that the food does not stick.
- Aluminum trays: Food is cooked in these disposable pans to prevent the fat dripping onto the charcoal and catching fire. They should be oiled to prevent the food from sticking. For the characteristic charcoal aroma, put the cooked food directly on the grid for a short time, turning once.

Some other useful accessories:

- A meat thermometer to measure the temperature inside large pieces of meat.
- Brushes for basting the food with oil or marinade.
- Metal and wooden skewers for making kebabs. The metal ones should be flat or notched so that the food is held firmly without rotating.
- A small shovel for adding charcoal.
- A wire brush for cleaning the grid and fire bowl.
- A bucket of water in case the fire gets out of control – it is always better to be safe than sorry!

Basic techniques

To ensure the best results when barbecuing, follow these important tips:

The grid

The grid should be placed about 2 to 3 in/5 to 7 cm above the fire. Before using the barbecue, the grid must be cleaned thoroughly and all burnt-on food and fat removed. If the grid is very dirty and encrusted with food and fat you can use a wire brush or crumpled up piece of foil. In order to prevent food from sticking, it is best to oil the grid with vegetable oil before you start cooking. Oil is better than butter, which burns more easily.

Temperature

The temperature of electric or gas barbecues can easily be controlled by turning the knob. Charcoal is a little trickier. If charcoal is too hot, push the pieces apart with a poker, or cook the food near the edge of the grid, where it will be cooler. If the temperature is too low, put the food to one side, knock the ash off the charcoal and increase the rate of combustion with a few puffs of the bellows.

Cooking in aluminum foil

If you want the food to brown on the outside, wrap it only very loosely in foil. To prevent the food from browning at all, wrap it tightly in foil.

Cooking in the charcoal embers

Food wrapped in foil can also be placed directly on the charcoal. Potatoes are particularly suitable for cooking in this way.

Cooking on a skewer

Food cooked on a skewer can be cooked very evenly since they are easy to turn. It is important that the food should be arranged evenly and stuck firmly on the skewer. Brush the meat frequently with fat or marinade during the cooking process.

Cooking methods

Grilling

This means cooking the food directly over the heat.

Sautéing

Food can be cooked on a barbecue in a heavy-based skillet (frying pan) in the same way as on an ordinary stove. The pan must be oiled well and the fire should be very hot. Do not use a pan with a wooden or plastic handle, which might be damaged by the heat.

Roasting

Large pieces of meat can be roasted by moving the charcoal to one side and enclosing the grid with a cover or lid so that the heat comes from all sides.

Barbecue food

Meat

Preserved and salted meat is not suitable for cooking on a barbecue. The curing salts may lead to the production of nitrosamines, which are carcinogenic substances. When buying meat, check that it has been well-hung.

There are many suitable cuts for cooking on the barbecue, including the following:

Pork: Chops, medallions, spareribs, tenderloin, loin, belly, knuckle, leg.

Veal: Sliced veal breast, cutlets, boneless rump roast, escalopes, fillet, steaks, rolled roast shoulder.

Beef: Sirloin, fillet, round (rump) steak, rib, topside joint.

Lamb: Chops, rolled shoulder, leg.

Poultry: Chicken breast, thighs, wings, chicken halves, whole chicken, turkey breast, turkey fillets, duck breast.

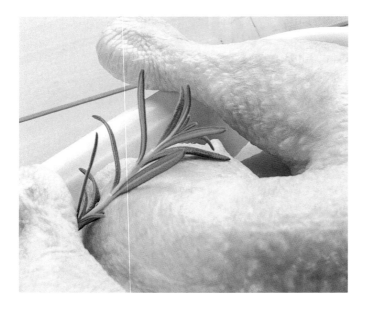

Preliminary preparation of meat

- Wash the pieces of meat and wipe dry with paper towels. Oil the meat well before putting it on the grid. This helps prevent the juices from escaping.
- A marinade made from oil and a mixture of herbs will give the meat a spicy aroma as well as make it more tender. The meat will absorb the marinade more quickly at room temperature than in the refrigerator. Small pieces of meat should be left to marinate for one or two hours, while larger pieces should be left in the refrigerator overnight.
- Beef steaks can be marinated for about 1 hour in pineapple juice. The effect of the enzymes in the pineapple juice is to tenderize the meat.
- Do not cover the meat with salt or dry herbs before cooking. Salt tends to dry out the meat, while herbs may add a bitter taste if burnt. To flavor the meat, sprinkle herbs directly on the fire.
- Prick sausages several times before cooking so that they do not burst.

Fish and seafood

Fish with firm flesh such as trout, bream, sea bass, shark, tuna, salmon, snapper, rose fish and whitefish are ideally suited for grilling on a barbecue, as are jumbo shrimps (prawns), crayfish, and squid. You can tell if fish is fresh by its shiny colour – fish that are less fresh have a rather lackluster appearance. The eyes must be clear and the scales should not become detached too easily.

Preparation of fish

- The fish must be gutted and scaled, and the gills and fins removed.
- The fish must be washed inside and out and wiped dry.
- If a fish weighs more than 1 lb/450 g, score it diagonally along the back two or three times so that it cooks evenly.
- A hinged metal fish grilling baskets is particularly good for barbecuing because it makes it easy to turn the fish without damaging it or causing it to fall apart. Oil the grilling basket before putting the fish inside so that it does not stick.

Beware of the risk of salmonella

The danger of salmonella is particularly great at the height of summer. If you are using deep-frozen fish, make sure that it has thawed completely, so that there is no risk of the middle being undercooked. Pour away the water resulting from defrosting, wash the fish thoroughly and wipe dry. Fresh fish must be put in the refrigerator immediately after purchase and only taken out just before cooking.

Vegetables and fruit

Barbecued vegetable and fruit dishes will not only appeal to vegetarians! Whether as a main dish or a side dish, there is no limit to the range of mouth-watering vegetable and fruit dishes that can be cooked on a barbecue. Delicious possibilities include corncobs and potatoes, sweet bell peppers, eggplants (aubergines), mushrooms, and tomatoes, cooked on skewers or wrapped in foil parcels.

As a dessert, fruit kebabs coated in honey and brown sugar are irresistible. They only need to be cooked on the barbecue for a few minutes.

Drinks

Don't forget the drinks you will be serving at the barbecue. It helps to make a list of all the drinks needed before the party, particularly if children will be there.

Put the drinks in the refrigerator the day before the party or ask the store to pre-chill them. Then keep them in insulated cool boxes with cooling bricks. They can also be kept cold for a shorter time in the cool bags available from supermarkets.

Make sure that you have enough ice cubes. If you run out of ice trays you can buy handy plastic ice cube bags from a supermarket.

Meat & Poultry

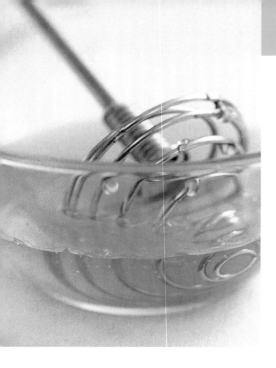

Sherry and honey spareribs

This is a sophisticated variation on the usual spareribs with spicy tomato sauce. The sherry marinade adds a piquant, aromatic note while the honey gives the spareribs a beautiful golden brown crusty coating.

3¼ lb/1.5 kg spareribs, cut into individual servings

2 cloves garlic

1 shallot

⅝ cup/5 fl oz/150 ml oil

½ cup/3½ fl oz/100 ml sherry

2 tablespoons oregano

1 teaspoon sugar

1 teaspoon salt

freshly ground white pepper

5 tablespoons honey

1 Wash the spareribs in running water and pat dry with paper towels. Put the meat to be marinated in a wide, shallow dish. Peel the cloves of garlic and shallots and chop finely. Add the oil, sherry, oregano, sugar, salt, and pepper. Stir together well.

2 Pour the marinade over the spareribs and turn these over in the marinade several times. Cover the dish with a lid or foil and stand in a cool place. Marinate for at least 24 hours.

3 Drain the ribs well and put on the grid (but not too close to the glowing charcoal!) and grill slowly. Turn several times and brush from to time to time with the remaining marinade.

4 After about 15 minutes coat the spareribs with honey and grill for a further 10 minutes until a beautiful crust has formed. Serve the spareribs with a bakery-style baguette and green salad.

Serves 4–5. Preparation time: about 20 minutes + 24 hours marinating

Exotic kebabs

Barbecue dishes should not be too heavy when eating outside on a hot summer's day. This particular dish is both light and exotic, with the tropical fruits adding a sweet, spicy touch to the kebabs.

1 Wash the beef in running water and pat dry with paper towels. Cut the meat into 1¼-in/3-cm cubes and sprinkle with lemon juice. Peel the papaya, remove the seeds and cut the flesh into cubes of about 1¼-in/3-cm. Cut the pineapple slices into eight pieces.

2 Thread the beef and veal cubes onto the skewers, alternating with pieces of fruit. Stir the cayenne pepper and pepper into the oil and brush the kebabs with this mixture.

3 Put foil on the grid to prevent the pieces of fruit from turning black. Place the kebabs along the edge of the grid where the temperature is lower. Grill for about 10–15 minutes, turning regularly and brushing with vegetable oil. Serve with fragrant rice.

Serves 4. Preparation time: about 40 minutes

9 oz/250 g beef
9 oz/250 g veal
2 tablespoons lemon juice
1 papaya
3 slices pineapple
2–3 tablespoons oil
1 pinch cayenne pepper
freshly ground white pepper

9 oz/250 g pork loin

7 oz/200 g beef loin

5 oz/150 g prosciutto (Parma ham), thinly sliced

oil for brushing

freshly ground black pepper

juice of 1 lemon

For the chili sauce:

1 clove garlic

1 tablespoons olive oil

1 red bell (sweet) pepper

14 oz/400 g tomato paste

1 dried chili pod

salt

Kebabs with chili sauce

Almost any kind of meat can be used for the kebabs but it should be slightly marbled with fat, because the grilling process always dries the meat out a little. The prosciutto (Parma ham) gives the dish a sophisticated flavor that is enhanced by the spicy chili sauce.

❶ First make the chili sauce. Peel and finely chop the clove of garlic, then fry gently in the olive oil. Cut the bell (sweet) pepper into half. Remove the stalk, seeds and white skin inside. Cut into thin strips and cook gently with the chopped garlic for about 3 minutes.

❷ Add the tomato paste. Chop the chili very finely and add to the sauce. Simmer for about 10 minutes and finally season with salt.

❸ Wash the meat in running water and pat dry with paper towels. Cut the meat into cubes 1¼-in/3-cm and wrap each cube in a piece of the ham. Thread the meat cubes on oiled metal kebab skewers, alternating the beef and the pork.

❹ Brush the kebabs with oil and put on the barbecue grid. Grill for about 6–8 minutes. Season the kebabs with freshly ground black pepper and sprinkle with lemon juice. Serve with the hot chili sauce and freshly baked white bread.

Serves 4–6. Preparation time: about 40 minutes

8 slices belly of pork,
    about ⅜ in/1 cm thick

salt

freshly ground black pepper

3 tablespoons Dijon or other
    mustard

1 teaspoon paprika

1 teaspoon ground caraway

1 tablespoon oil

½ cup/4 fl oz/125 ml dark beer

Crisp belly of pork

A straightforward barbecued dish that will be less fatty if the leaner part of the belly of pork is used. This cut is ideally suited to grilling and does not require much seasoning. Here is an easy trick to get it beautifully crisp: brush it with beer! The dish is delicious served with grilled slices of zucchini.

❶ Make several cuts into the rind and season the meat with salt and pepper. Add the mustard, paprika powder, and caraway to the oil and stir. Coat the meat with this mixture and leave covered in a cool place for 30 minutes.

❷ Cover the grid with foil to prevent the fat from dripping into the fire. Grill the belly of pork slices for about 5 minutes on each side. Then brush with beer and grill for another 2 minutes on each side until crisp.

Serves 4. Preparation time: about 10 minutes + 30 minutes marinating

Spicy seasoned pork chops

As well as being a traditional part of Oriental dishes, spices from the Far East such as cumin or turmeric also make delicious marinades for grilled meat. So that the meat will absorb all the flavors, it is worth starting to marinate the meat the day before it is to be cooked.

❶ Peel and finely chop the cloves of garlic. Crush the peppercorns coarsely in a mortar. Put the chopped garlic, pepper, lemon juice and 3 tablespoonfuls of soy sauce in a bowl and stir well. Add the cumin, turmeric, cardamom, cinnamon and cayenne pepper and stir again.

❷ Wash the pork chops in running water and pat dry with paper towels. Put the pork chops in a shallow dish and pour over the marinade. Turn the chops over in the marinade so that they are well coated. Cover the dish with a lid or foil and leave in the refrigerator overnight.

❸ Stir the maple syrup into the rest of the soy sauce mixture. Take the chops out of the marinade, drain well and grill slowly over medium heat, turning them several times. After about 15 minutes brush with the maple syrup and soy sauce mixture. Grill for a further 5 minutes on each side. The dish is excellent served with steamed rice.

Serves 4. Preparation time: about 15 minutes + 12 hours marinating

2 cloves garlic

10 white peppercorns

juice of 1 lemon

5 tablespoons dark soy sauce

¼ teaspoon ground caraway

½ teaspoon ground turmeric

¼ teaspoon ground cardamom

½ teaspoon ground cinnamon

1 pinch cayenne pepper

2 tablespoons peanut
   (groundnut) oil

3¼ lb/1.5 kg pork chops

2 tablespoons maple syrup

Grilled meat with spicy apricot sauce

This fruity sauce will make any grilled meat beautifully tender. It is brushed onto the chicken, pork and veal before grilling and left to soak in for about one hour, thus enabling the Oriental ingredients to develop their full flavor.

4 chicken breast fillets

4 pork chops

4 veal cutlets

1 large, ripe apricot

½ ripe papaya

1 tablespoon dark rum

1 tablespoon sugar

2 tablespoons soy sauce

1 tablespoon freshly grated ginger

1–2 teaspoons sambal oelek

1 teaspoon caraway

freshly ground black pepper

1 tablespoon tomato paste

❶ Wash the chicken breast fillets in running water and pat dry with paper towels. Put the meat in a shallow dish. Pour boiling water over the apricots, remove the skin, cut into half and remove the pit (stone). Peel the papaya and remove the seeds. Cut the flesh of the papaya and apricots into small pieces.

❷ Put the fruit pieces in a tall beaker together with the sugar, rum, soy sauce, ginger, sambal oelek, caraway, pepper, and tomato paste. Puree with a hand-mixer or in a blender to make a paste. Coat the meat on all sides with the fruit paste, pour the rest over the meat and put in a cool place.

❸ Place the pieces of meat on the grid and grill for 5–10 minutes. Turn the chicken breast fillets and veal cutlets once and the pork chops several times. Serve the mixed grilled meats with crisp, farm-baked bread and potato salad.

Serves 4. Preparation time: about 25 minutes + 1 hour marinating

American hamburger steaks

A real delicacy for which only the best beef should be used. When selecting the cut, make sure that the meat is not too lean but contains about 20% fat. The meat can be ground (minced) at home, or the butcher can be asked to do it.

1¼ lb/600 g beef, such as round (rump steak)

freshly ground mixed colored pepper

1 clove garlic

4 tomatoes

1 teaspoon oregano

oil

sea salt

❶ Remove all the sinews and gristle but do not cut off the fatty edges. Cut the meat into large pieces and put it through the grinder but do not grind too finely.

❷ Put the ground beef in a dish and season with pepper. Peel the clove of garlic, chop finely and stir into the meat. Mould the meat mixture into four round hamburger steaks about 1¼ in/3 cm thick. Press the steaks into shape and cover with plastic wrap.

❸ Blanch the tomatoes in boiling water, make a cross-shaped cut in the end and peel off the skins. Season with oregano and colored pepper and sprinkle with a little oil.

❹ Brush the hamburger steaks with oil on both sides. Oil the barbecue grid, then grill the meat for about 4–6 minutes on each side. The meat should be crisp on the outside and juicy inside. Put the tomatoes on a piece of foil on the edge of the grid and cook over medium heat for about 5 minutes. Only season the hamburgers and tomatoes with sea salt once they are cooked.

Serves 4. Preparation time: about 35 minutes

Ground meat kebabs with yogurt dip

This spicy grilled dish of ground (minced) meat makes a delicious meal. The addition of nuts and porridge oats gives these small meatball kebabs a pleasant crispy bite. They are delicious served with an aromatic herb yogurt dip.

1 Put the ground meat in a dish, peel the shallot, chop finely, and add to the meat. Stir in the shallot, egg yolk, porridge oats and filberts (hazelnuts). Season the meat mixture with the herbs, salt and pepper.

2 Form the meat into balls of about 1¼ in/3 cm, press to flatten them slightly and thread 3 meatballs on each oiled metal skewer. Brush the meatballs with oil, cover the grid with foil and grill the kebabs for 10–15 minutes over medium heat.

3 Meanwhile make the dip. Stir the low-fat soft cheese (quark) and yogurt together. Peel and finely chop the garlic. Add to the cheese and yogurt mixture together with the parsley and chives. Season with salt and pepper. Serve the meat hot with pitta bread.

Serves 4. Preparation time: about 15 minutes

9 oz/250 g ground (minced) lamb

9 oz/250 g ground (minced) beef

1 shallot

1 egg yolk

1 tablespoon rolled oats

1 tablespoon coarsely chopped filberts (hazelnuts)

1 teaspoon herbes de Provence, or a mixture of dried thyme, basil and rosemary

salt

freshly ground white pepper

2 tablespoons oil

For the yogurt dip:

7 oz/200 g skimmed milk yogurt

2 tablespoons low-fat soft cheese (quark)

1 clove garlic

2 tablespoons chopped parsley

2 tablespoons chopped chives

salt

freshly ground black pepper

Colorful sausage kebabs

Sausages of every kind are very popular for barbecues. Served with vegetables, they make a delicious meal and have become a traditional barbecue dish. Depending on what is in the refrigerator, sausage-based barbecues can be varied endlessly.

10 thin sausages

1 red bell (sweet) pepper

1 zucchini

oil

1 pinch cayenne pepper

freshly ground mixed colored
   pepper

❶ Cut the sausages into two or three pieces about 2 in/5 cm long. Cut the red bell (sweet) pepper in half. Remove the stalk, seeds and white skin inside. Cut the pepper into broad strips and cut the zucchini into slices ⅜ in/1 cm thick .

❷ Thread the sausages, strips of pepper and zucchini slices alternately on oiled skewers. Brush with oil and season with cayenne pepper and pepper. Grill the skewers on each side for about 4 minutes.

Serves 4. Preparation time: about 10 minutes

Sausage and salami rolls

6 medium sausages

6 large slices salami

2 thin slices Swiss cheese

❶ Place each sausage on a slice of salami. Cut the Swiss cheese into thin strips and put 2 or 3 strips next to the sausage. Roll the salami round the sausage and secure with wooden cocktail sticks. Grill for about 8 minutes, turning several times.

Serves 3–4. Preparation time: about 10 minutes

Mushroom and sausage kebab

4 frankfurters

1 onion

3½ oz/100 g small mushrooms

1 teaspoon curry powder

1 teaspoon mustard

1 tablespoon oil

❶ Cut the frankfurters into pieces ¾ in/2 cm long. Peel the onion and cut into eight pieces. Clean the mushrooms. Thread the sausage, onion pieces and mushrooms alternately on oiled skewers.

❷ Stir together the curry, mustard and oil and brush the kebabs with this mixture. Grill over medium heat for about 7 minutes, turning several times.

Serves 4–6. Preparation time: about 10 minutes

Sausages wrapped in bacon

Sausages and bacon make deliciously tasty kebabs, served with nourishing black bread and a cool beer.

6 veal or pork sausages
paprika
6 slices bacon
2 tablespoons oil
12 cherry tomatoes
freshly ground white pepper

❶ Sprinkle the sausages with paprika and roll each one in a slice of bacon.

❷ Thread the sausages on oiled skewers and put a cherry tomato at each end. Brush the tomatoes with oil and season the kebabs with pepper. Grill over medium heat for about 8 minutes and turn carefully several times.

Serves 3. Preparation time: about 10 minutes

Barbecued hot dogs

To prevent the skins splitting while cooking, it is a good idea to dip the frankfurters in boiling water for a few seconds first. Then dry them on the grid before cooking.

4 frankfurters
oil
4 hot dog buns
tomato catsup (ketchup)
mustard
fried onions

❶ Brush the frankfurters with oil, put on the grid and cook for about 5 minutes, turning several times. Cut the hot dog buns lengthways, open them out and toast lightly on the grid, with the cut side downwards.

❷ Put the frankfurters in the rolls. Spread each one with tomato catsup, mustard and a spoonful of fried onions.

Serves 4. Preparation time: about 5 minutes

Barbecued stuffed sausages

The onions and garlic add a spicy touch for those who enjoy a tasty dish. The sausages must be served piping hot, so they are best served still wrapped in the foil.

1 Make a slit lengthways in each sausage. Peel and finely chop the onions and garlic very finely and cut the chives into very short cylindrical pieces. Add to the oil together with paprika and stir well.

2 Distribute the onion mixture evenly onto the opened-up sausages. Wrap the sausages in foil and grill for about 10 minutes.

Serves 4. Preparation time: about 10 minutes

4 thick sausages

2 onions

2 cloves garlic

1 bunch chives

1 teaspoon ground paprika

2 tablespoons oil

Barbecued steaks
with herb butter

4 beef steaks

2 cloves garlic

8 mixed colored peppercorns

1 teaspoon rosemary

1 teaspoon thyme

juice of 1 lime

1 teaspoon paprika

4 tablespoons oil

For the side dish:

18 oz/500 g potatoes

coarse sea salt

9 oz/250 g tomatoes

4 sprigs fresh rosemary

freshly ground black pepper

3 tablespoons oil

For the herb butter:

1 clove garlic

⅝ cup/5 oz/125 g butter

1 teaspoon chopped chives

1 teaspoon chopped cress

1 teaspoon chervil

Juicy grilled steaks are a classic barbecue dish. A few points are essential to success: always buy top-quality meat, and when grilling, sear quickly so as to seal in the juices, then cook slowly according to taste.

1 Wash the beef steaks in running water and pat dry with paper towels. Put the steaks in a shallow dish. Peel the garlic and crush coarsely with the peppercorns in a mortar. Add the herbs, lime juice, paprika powder and oil. Stir well and pour the marinade over the steaks. Turn the meat several times so that it is well coated. Cover with plastic wrap and leave in the refrigerator for about 4 hours.

2 Clean the potatoes with a brush, cut in half and boil for about 7 minutes in a little salted water. Wash the tomatoes and remove the stalks. Cut the tomatoes in half. Put the potatoes and tomatoes in an aluminum foil pan and arrange the sprigs of rosemary on top. Season with salt and freshly ground pepper and pour the oil on top.

3 For the herb butter, peel and crush the clove of garlic. Add to the softened butter and stir in the herbs with a fork. Put the herb butter in the refrigerator.

4 Remove the steaks from the marinade and drain well. Cook them briefly over high heat on both sides, then move them to the side of the grid. Put the foil pan containing the tomatoes and potatoes on the grid and cook with the steaks for about another 10 minutes.

5 Remove the steaks from the grid, arrange with the potatoes and tomatoes on plates and put a knob of herb butter on each steak.

Serves 4. Preparation time: about 30 minutes + 4 hours marinating

Stuffed veal rolls

A sophisticated dish based on a recipe originally from Italy. This variation is particularly quick to prepare and makes a welcome change to more traditional barbecue dishes.

6 thin veal escalopes

freshly ground white pepper

4 tablespoons oil

1 tablespoon lemon juice

1 teaspoon thyme

5 oz/150 g ricotta or soft curd cheese

2 tablespoons chopped parsley

12 slices prosciutto (Parma ham)

1 Wash the escalopes of veal in running water and pat dry with paper towels. Put the escalopes of veal in a shallow dish and season with pepper. Add the lemon juice and thyme to the oil to make a marinade. Pour over the meat, cover, and leave in the refrigerator for 2 hours.

2 Remove the veal from the marinade and drain well. Stir the chopped parsley into the ricotta. Put 2 slices of ham on each escalope and place 1 or 2 teaspoons of ricotta on top. Roll up each escalope and secure with small wooden skewers or cocktail sticks.

3 Grill the rolled escalopes over medium heat for about 5–8 minutes, turning them carefully now and again.

Serves 4. Preparation time: about 15 minutes + 2 hours marinating

Steaks with a soft cheese and lime dip

These thin steaks are not only very quick to prepare but also ideal for calorie-conscious guests. The delicate sharpness of the limes adds a deliciously refreshing touch to the dip.

1 Stir together the low-fat soft cheese (quark), yogurt and lime juice until smooth. Chop the basil leaves finely and stir into the cheese mixture. Season the dip with pepper.

2 Wash the beef steaks in running water and pat dry with paper towels. Brush the steaks with oil, season with pepper and grill for about 2 minutes on both sides. Wash parsley and pat dry with paper towels. Chop the parsley very finely. Remove the steaks from the barbecue, season lightly with salt, and sprinkle the parsley on top. Serve with the cheese and lime dip, white bread and a light white wine.

Serves 4. Preparation time: about 10 minutes

7 oz/200 g low-fat soft cheese (quark)

2 tablespoons yogurt

juice of 1 lime

about 10 leaves fresh basil

freshly ground white pepper

4 thin beef steaks, cut about $\frac{3}{16}$ in/5 mm thick

oil

½ bunch parsley

salt

Glazed chicken wings

With their shiny crisp skin, these chicken wings with baked potatoes make a delicious barbecue

1 For the marinade, peel the garlic peels and put through a garlic press. Mix with the catsup, balsamic vinegar, lime juice, paprika, chilli pepper, honey, brown sugar, Tabasco, salt and pepper to make a smooth paste.

2 Wash the chicken wings and pat dry. Spread with the marinade, cover and leave to stand for about 30 minutes.

3 Put the chicken wings on the grid and grill for about 15 minutes until the meat done. Brush again with the marinade so that the chicken wings are glazed.

Serves 4. Preparation time: about 5 minutes + 30 minutes marinating

2 cloves of garlic

4 tablespoons tomato catsup (ketchup)

2 tablespoons balsamic vinegar

juice of 2 limes

1 teaspoons strong paprika

½ teaspoon chilli pepper

3 tablespoons honey

1 tablespoon brown sugar

several dashes Tabasco

salt

freshly ground black pepper

20 chicken wings

Beef sirloin in a red wine marinade

A barbecue dish that can replace the traditional Sunday roast. Slices of beef are marinated in a sophisticated red wine marinade, which is then used to make a spicy sauce. It is delicious served with sauté potatoes and a mixed salad.

8 slices beef sirloin,
  about ⅜ in/1 cm thick

½ teaspoon salt

freshly ground black pepper

1 clove garlic

1 tablespoon capers

1 chili pod

4 preserved anchovy fillets

1 teaspoon thyme

2 bay leaves

1¾ cups/14 fl oz/400 ml red wine

3 tablespoons olive oil

1 tablespoon cornstarch
  (cornflour)

3½ oz/100 g crème fraîche

❶ Wash the beef in running water and pat dry with paper towels. Put the meat in a large shallow dish and season with salt and pepper. Peel the clove of garlic and chop finely together with the capers. Cut the chili lengthways, remove the seeds and cut into thin strips.

❷ Remove the bones from the anchovy fillets and chop finely. Sprinkle the chopped anchovy, garlic, capers, chili, thyme, and bay leaves over the beef, then pour the red wine on top. Cover with a lid or foil and leave in the refrigerator for about 12 hours.

❸ Remove the meat from the marinade and drain well. Barbecue the slices on each side for 3 to 4 minutes.

❹ Meanwhile prepare the sauce. Remove the bay leaves from the marinade, pour the liquid into a pan and bring to the boil. Add 1–2 tablespoons of cold water into the cornstarch (cornflour), stir well, and add to the simmering marinade, stirring continuously.

❺ Remove the sauce from the heat and puree with a hand-mixer or in a blender. Stir in the crème fraîche and season with salt and pepper. Arrange the grilled meat on plates and pour over the sauce.

Serves 6. Preparation time: about 25 minutes + 12 hours marinating

Lamb cutlets with mint

The meat becomes very tender and full of flavor as a result of the marinade and is therefore ideal for grilling. The delicious fragrance of the mint perfectly complements the natural taste of the lamb.

❶ Put the lamb cutlets in a shallow dish. Peel and finely chop the clove of garlic and sprinkle over the meat. Pour the port, oil and lemon juice over all.

❷ Put a few mint leaves aside for the garnish. Chop the rest finely and sprinkle over the meat. Turn the cutlets over in the marinade several times. Cover the dish and leave in the refrigerator for 3 hours.

❸ Remove the cutlets from the marinade and drain well. Grill on each side for about 6 minutes. After grilling, season with salt and pepper and garnish with mint leaves.

Serves 6. Preparation time: about 10 minutes + 3 hours marinating

6 lamb cutlets

1 clove garlic

2 tablespoons port wine

2 tablespoons oil

juice of 1 lemon

2 sprigs mint

salt

freshly ground black pepper

Some lamb variations

Lamb can be prepared in many ways. It is a very popular meat in the countries of the Mediterranean, which are the source of these delicious suggestions.

Slices of lamb in red wine

6 slices lamb from the leg

2 cloves garlic

1 tablespoon oregano

3 sprigs rosemary

freshly ground black pepper

½ cup/4 fl oz/125 ml red wine

3 tablespoons oil

salt

❶ Wash the slices of lamb in running water and pat dry with paper towels. Arrange the slices of lamb in a shallow dish. Peel and crush the cloves of garlic and rub onto the meat. Season with the oregano and pepper, then put the sprigs of rosemary on top. Pour the red wine over the meat, cover the dish, and leave in the refrigerator for 3 hours.

❷ Remove the meat from the marinade and drain well. Brush both sides with oil and grill for about 8 minutes, turning once. Season with salt and pepper after grilling and serve with sauté potatoes and a yogurt and garlic dip (page 29).

Serves 6. Preparation time: about 10 minutes + 3 hours marinating

Lamb cutlets with herbes de Provence

6 lamb cutlets

1 shallot

10 mixed colored peppercorns

1 tablespoon herbes de Provence or a mixture of dried thyme, basil and rosemary

4 tablespoons oil

salt

❶ Put the cutlets in a shallow dish. Peel the shallot and cut into eight pieces. Put in a mortar together with the peppercorns and herbs and crush coarsely. Coat the meat with this mixture.

❷ Pour the oil over the meat and leave to stand in the refrigerator for 12 hours. Remove the meat from the marinade. Grill the meat for 5 minutes on each side. After grilling, season with salt and serve with garlic bread.

Serves 6. Preparation time: about 10 minutes + 12 hours marinating

Lamb kebabs with parsley and lemon marinade

18 oz/500 g slices of lamb from
  the leg

2 lemons

1 bunch smooth parsley

freshly ground white pepper

4 tablespoons oil

5 shallots

The addition of lemon and parsley make this lamb dish quite irresistible. The kebabs are quite easy to prepare, but it is important to marinate the meat for the time stated so that the flavors of the individual ingredients can merge together.

❶ Wash the slices of lamb in running water and pat dry with paper towels. Cut the meat into cubes of about 1¼ in/3 cm and put in a shallow dish. Slice 1 of the lemons and squeeze the other. Put the slices of lemon on the meat and pour the juice on top.

❷ Put a few parsley leaves to one side for the garnish. Wash the rest and pat dry with paper towels. Chop finely and sprinkle over the meat together with the pepper. Pour over the oi. Put in the refrigerator for 5 hours.

❸ Remove the meat from the marinade and drain well. Peel the shallots, cut in half and thread on the oiled skewers, alternating with the cubes of meat. Grill for about 7 minutes, turning several times. Garnish the kebabs with parsley.

Serves 4–6. Preparation time: about 10 minutes + 5 hours marinating

Grilled chicken with herb oil

A juicy roast chicken flavored with aromatic herbs is absolutely delicious. The chicken is simply cut in half and grilled. The chicken should be continually basted with herb oil.

1 Wash the chickens in running water. Remove the backbone and cut in half. Pat dry with paper towels.

2 Put the sea salt, peppercorns, oregano, marjoram and rosemary in a mortar and crush as finely as possible. Stir the oil into the herb mixture and brush the chicken halves with it on all sides.

3 Put the rosemary twigs on the glowing charcoal – the rising fragrance will enhance the herbal aroma. Put the chicken halves on the oiled grid and cook for about 30 minutes, turning several times and basting regularly with the remaining herb oil. Check to see if the chicken is cooked by pricking the thigh with a fork. When the juices run clear the chicken is ready.

Serves 4. Preparation time: about 15 minutes

**2 small chickens
   (about 2½ lb/1.2 kg each)**

1 teaspoon coarse sea salt

10 white peppercorns

1 tablespoon oregano

1 tablespoon marjoram

1 tablespoon rosemary

6 tablespoons oil

3 sprigs fresh rosemary

Chicken thighs with creamed avocado

Chicken is relatively low in fat so the marinade should always contain some oil. To ensure the skin is beautifully crisp, sprinkle salt over the chicken before grilling. It is delicious served with a mild creamed avocado sauce.

4 chicken thighs

1 teaspoon curry powder

2 tablespoons soy sauce

1 tablespoon sherry

3 tablespoons oil

1 tablespoon ground coriander

sea salt

2 ripe avocados

2 tablespoons lemon juice

freshly ground white pepper

1 tablespoon crème fraîche

1 tablespoon chervil

2 tablespoons salted cashew nuts

❶ Wash the chicken thighs in running water and pat dry with paper towels. Put the chicken thighs in a shallow dish. Mix together the curry, soy sauce, sherry, oil, and fresh chopped coriander. Pour the marinade over the chicken thighs. Cover and stand in the refrigerator for 3 hours.

❷ Remove the chicken thighs from the marinade, drain, sprinkle salt on top, put in a disposable aluminum foil pan, and grill over medium heat for about 15–20 minutes until golden brown.

❸ Cut the avocados in half, remove the pit (stone), scoop out the flesh with a spoon, and sprinkle with lemon juice to prevent it from going brown.

❹ Mash the avocado flesh with a fork into a cream and stir in the freshly ground white pepper, crème fraîche and finely chopped chervil. Chop the cashew nuts coarsely and sprinkle over the avocado mixture. Serve the chicken wings and creamed avocado with a baguette and white wine.

Serves 4. Preparation time: about 15 minutes + 3 hours marinating

Chicken saté kebabs

Chicken saté kebabs served with a sweet and spicy peanut sauce are ideal for an exotic barbecue evening. Garam masala can be found in Oriental food shops.

14 oz/400 g chicken breast fillets

2 onions

1 tablespoon fresh ginger, grated

9 tablespoons coconut milk

2 tablespoons yogurt

3 tablespoons garam masala (mixed spices)

3 tablespoons smooth peanut butter

4 tablespoons coconut milk

2 tablespoons lemon juice

1 tablespoon flaked (desiccated) coconut

1 pinch cayenne pepper

1 pinch caraway

oil for the kebabs

❶ Wash the chicken breast fillets in running water and pat dry with paper towels. Cut the chicken fillets into cubes of ¾ in/2 cm. Peel the onions and chop finely. Add to the yogurt together with the ginger, 5 tablespoons coconut milk and garam masala. Stir the meat cubes into the marinade and leave to stand in the refrigerator for 1 hour.

❷ Thread the meat cubes onto oiled wooden skewers and grill for about 6–8 minutes over medium heat, turning several times.

❸ To make the sauce, mix together the peanut butter, 4 tablespoons coconut milk, lemon juice and flaked coconut. Stir vigorously. Season with cayenne pepper and cumin. Serve this sauce with the hot kebabs.

Serves 4. Preparation time: about 15 minutes + 1 hour marinating

Chicken wings

Chicken wings coated with spicy chili sauce have become a barbecue classic. If any are left over, they are ideal for a picnic.

❶ Wash the chicken wings and pat dry. Peel the onions and cloves of garlic and chop very finely. Cut the chili in half, remove the seeds and chop finely.

❷ Add the chopped onions, cloves of garlic, chili, and paprika to the tomato paste. Stir in 1–2 tablespoons of hot water and balsamic vinegar. Season with sugar, salt and freshly ground pepper.

❸ Brush the chicken wings with the chili sauce and stand in the refrigerator for about 1 hour. Line the barbecue grid with foil and grill the chicken wings for about 10 minutes, turning several times. Serve the chicken wings with baked potatoes and grilled corncobs.

Serves 4. Preparation time: about 10 minutes + 1 hour marinating

12 chicken wings

2 onions

2 cloves garlic

1 chili pod

1 teaspoon paprika

3 tablespoons tomato paste

1 tablespoon balsamic vinegar

½ teaspoon sugar

½ teaspoon salt

freshly ground white pepper

Turkey escalopes with sage

The turkey escalopes are steeped in a sharp marinade of yogurt and mustard that gives the meat a delicious tang. The sage and scallions (spring onions) with which they are stuffed enhance the delicate flavor.

❶ Wash the turkey breasts and pat them dry. Using a sharp knife, cut a pocket in the side of each turkey escalope. Clean and finely chop the scallions (spring onions). Wash the sage leaves and shake dry. Mix with the scallions and spoon into each pocket. Close the pockets with wooden toothpicks.

❷ Stir together the yogurt, mustard, oil, pepper and nutmeg. Put the escalopes in a flat dish and spread the marinade over both sides of each one. Cover and leave to marinate in a cool place for about 2 hours.

❸ Cover the grid with metal foil. Grill the escalopes over medium heat for about 10–12 minutes, turning several times while cooking. When done, spread with any remaining marinade.

Serves 4. Preparation time: about 10 minutes + 2 hours marinating

4 turkey-scraps

4 scallions (spring onions)

12 fresh sage-leaves

3 tablespoons yogurt

1 tablespoon sharp mustard

1 tablespoon oil

freshly ground mixed colored pepper

1 pinch ground nutmeg

Chicken with a Parmesan cheese crust

Chicken is very versatile food and can be prepared in a variety of ways to suit every taste. In this sophisticated recipe, the chicken thighs are coated with a spicy paste of Parmesan cheese and chervil, then grilled until deliciously crisp.

8 chicken thighs

3 cloves garlic

1 teaspoon coarse sea salt

3 eggs

1 tablespoon lemon juice

1 pinch ground nutmeg

freshly ground white pepper

5 tablespoons oil

¾ cup/2 oz/50 g dried white breadcrumbs

⅓ cup/2 oz/50 g grated Parmesan cheese

2 tablespoons chervil

1 tablespoon tarragon

oil for sprinkling

❶ Wash the chicken thighs, pat dry and place in a shallow dish. Peel the cloves of garlic and crush together with the coarse sea salt in a mortar. Carefully whisk together the garlic paste, eggs, lemon juice, nutmeg and pepper with a fork.

❷ Pour the egg mixture over the chicken thighs and turn them, ensuring they are well coated. Cover and leave in the refrigerator for 4 hours.

❸ Stir the breadcrumbs, Parmesan cheese, finely chopped chervil, and tarragon into the oil. Put this paste on a large plate and roll the chicken thighs in it, pressing lightly to make sure the paste sticks to the thighs. Place the chicken thighs in a disposable aluminum foil pan, sprinkle a little oil on top and grill for about 30 minutes, turning carefully throughout. Serve with grilled vegetables.

Serves 4. Preparation time: about 15 minutes + 4 hours marinating

Chicken in a peanut crust

The crisp chicken pieces are coated in a peanut paste, inspired by Oriental cuisine. This gives the chicken a slightly sweet, nutty flavor.

❶ Wash the chicken and pat dry. Using poultry shears, cut the chicken into 8 portions. Arrange these in a shallow dish. Mix together the peanut oil and lemon juice, pour over the chicken and turn the pieces over so that they are well coated. Place in the refrigerator for 4 hours.

❷ Prepare three mixtures for the coating. For the first, mix together the cornstarch (cornflour), curry, saffron, turmeric and pepper in a large, shallow gratin dish. For the second, stir together the peanut butter, coriander leaves and yogurt and pour this mixture onto a plate. Lastly, season the eggs with salt, whisk with the coconut milk, and pour onto another plate.

❸ First coat the chicken thighs with the cornstarch mixture, then with the peanut mixture, then with the egg mixture. Finally coat again in the cornstarch mixture. Put the chicken thighs in an oiled aluminum foil pan, pour a little peanut oil on top and grill for about 25–30 minutes, turning from time to time.

Serves 4. Preparation time: about 25 minutes + 4 hours marinating

1 chicken

5 tablespoons peanut (groundnut) oil

2 tablespoons lemon juice

¾ cup 3½ oz/100 g cornstarch (cornflour)

1 tablespoon curry powder

1 pinch saffron

1 teaspoon turmeric

freshly ground mixed colored pepper

3 tablespoons peanut butter

2 tablespoons fresh coriander leaves

2 tablespoons yogurt

2 eggs

salt

4 tablespoons coconut milk

peanut (groundnut) oil

49

Shashlik and cevapcici

Shashlik is the name for Russian kebabs, while cevapcici describes a kind of meatball. The combination is excellent with pickled vegetables, fresh white bread, and a cucumber and yogurt dip.

For the shashlik kebabs:

18 oz/500 g lean pork

3 onions

3 slices smoked belly of pork, about ⅜ in/1 cm thick

2 small zucchini

salt

freshly ground black pepper

½ chili pod, finely chopped

1 teaspoon ground paprika

½ cup/4 fl oz/125 ml oil

For the cevapcici:

18 oz/500 g ground (minced) lamb

1 tablespoon breadcrumbs

1 clove garlic

1 egg yolk

1 teaspoon oregano

freshly ground black pepper

salt

2 tablespoons oil

❶ For the kebabs, wash the pork in running water, pat dry with paper towels and cut into cubes of about 1¼ in/3 cm. Peel and quarter the onions. Cut the smoked belly of pork into pieces 1¼ in/3 cm square. Wash the zucchini and cut into slices ⅜ in/1 cm thick. Put all the ingredients in a flat dish.

❷ Mix the salt, pepper, chili pod, ground paprika and oil together. Pour the marinade over the meat and vegetables. Cover and let stand for about 2 hours.

❸ Drain the meat and vegetables, then thread alternately on the skewers.

❹ For the cevapcici, put the ground (minced) lamb and breadcrumbs in a bowl. Peel and finely chop the clove of garlic. Add it to the meat with the egg yolk, oregano, pepper and salt and stir together.

❺ Using the hands, mix the meat and other ingredients into a smooth paste, then mould it into sausage-shaped lengths about ¾ in/2 cm thick. Sprinkle with oil. Put the shashlik kebabs on the grid and cook for about 3 minutes. Then add the cevapcici and cook all for 3–5 minutes, turning from time to time.

Serves 6. Preparation time: about 30 minutes + 2 hours marinating

Ground lamb Asian style

Here ground (minced) lamb is prepared in an unusual way. The delicate, exotic spices and the crisp peanuts give the meat a marvelously piquant flavor. It is delicious served with steamed fragrant rice.

1 Put the coriander seeds, caraway and turmeric in a small pan without oil and toast lightly for 2 minutes, shaking the pan from time to time. Put in a mortar and pound the spices until fine.

2 Add the spices to the ground (minced) lamb. Finely chop the shallots, garlic and ginger. Add to the meat with the lemon juice, chili pepper, pepper and salt. Chop the peanuts finely and add to the mixture.

3 Knead the lamb with the other ingredients, pressing the mixture firmly together. Form into 12 little rolls. Put 3 on each oiled skewer. Place the skewers on a large dish and cover with plastic wrap. Let stand for 3 hours.

4 Moisten the meat with peanut (groundnut) oil and grill for about 5 minutes. Wash the coriander leaves, shake dry and chop finely. Sprinkle on the skewers before serving.

Serves 4. Preparation time: about 15 minutes + 3 hours marinating

1 teaspoon coriander seeds

1 teaspoon caraway

1 teaspoon turmeric

14 oz/400 g ground (minced) lamb (from the neck, lightly marbled)

2 shallots

2 cloves garlic

1 small piece fresh ginger

2 tablespoons lemon juice

½ teaspoon chili pepper

freshly ground mixed colored pepper

1 pinch sea salt

1 cup/3½ oz/100 g salted peanuts

3 tablespoons peanut (groundnut) oil

2 tablespoons chopped fresh coriander

Fish & Shellfish

4 cod fillets

3 tablespoons lemon juice

3 tablespoons olive oil

1 teaspoon oregano

1 teaspoon thyme

freshly ground black pepper

1 eggplant (aubergine)

salt

2 tomatoes

12 black olives

Fish fillet with eggplants (aubergines) and olives

This barbecue dish evokes images of sunny climes – at least from a culinary point of view – with its olives, tomatoes and herbs.

❶ Rinse the fish fillets briefly in cold water and pat dry with paper towels. Mix the lemon juice, olive oil, oregano, thyme and pepper together. Brush the fish with this marinade. Put in a dish, cover and leave in the refrigerator for 1 hour.

❷ Wash the eggplant (aubergine) and remove the stalk. Cut the eggplant into thin slices, sprinkle with salt, and leave in a cool place for 20 minutes to draw out the water. Pat the slices dry with paper towels. Wash the tomatoes, remove the stalks and cut the tomatoes into thin slices. Cut the olives in half and remove the pits (stones).

❸ Place the fish fillets on pieces of foil of the appropriate size. Arrange the eggplant slices, tomatoes and olives on top. Sprinkle with the rest of the marinade and seal the parcels. Grill the fish parcels over medium heat for about 10 minutes. Arrange the parcels on the plates and serve immediately.

Serves 4. Preparation time: about 40 minutes + 1 hour marinating

Traditional grilled trout

Trout is ideally suited for the barbecue. It can be prepared in a variety of ways, such as grilling in a hinged fish grilling basket, oiled so that the skin does not stick. On the other hand, cooking in sealed foil parcels is the ideal way of preserving the trout's delicate flavor.

Barbecued trout

4 trout
juice of 2 lemons
sea salt
freshly ground black pepper
1 bunch dill
oil
1 sprig dried thyme
some green fennel

❶ Wash the trout under running water and pat dry with paper towels. Sprinkle the fish inside and out with lemon juice and season with salt and pepper.

❷ Chop the dill finely and put inside the trout. Brush the fish with oil and place in the oiled fish grilling basket.

❸ Place the sprigs of thyme and fennel leaves on the charcoal to scent the smoke and grill the fish for about 6 minutes on each side.

Serves 4. Preparation time: about 10 minutes

Trout in foil

4 trout
juice of 2 lemons
sea salt
freshly ground black pepper
1 bunch parsley
⅝ cup/5 oz/150 g butter
18 oz/500 g large potatoes
3½ oz/100 g crème fraîche

❶ Prepare the trout in the same way as the previous recipe and season with lemon juice, salt and pepper. Wash the parsley and pat dry with paper towels. Chop the parsley finely and put inside the trout together with a teaspoon of butter.

❷ Butter 4 large pieces of extra strong foil and wrap the fish loosely in it.

❸ Clean the potatoes with a brush under running water and cut in half. Butter pieces of foil and place a potato on each. Season with pepper, dot with the remaining butter and wrap up in the foil.

❹ Cook the fish and potatoes on the grill for about 35 minutes, turning the trout carefully from time to time. Open up the foil containing the potatoes and put a teaspoon of crème fraîche on each one. Sprinkle a little salt on top. Arrange the trout and potatoes on large plates.

Serves 4. Preparation time: about 20 minutes

Tarragon trout

A mouthwatering combination of ingredients that will appeal to everyone. The delicate flavors of the tarragon and fennel add a touch of sophistication to this dish.

1 Wash the trout and pat dry. Season with salt inside and out.

2 Peel the cloves of garlic and chop finely. Clean and wash the fennel. Grate finely and mix with the finely chopped tarragon and garlic. Place inside the trout and secure with cocktail sticks.

3 Brush the outside of the trout with oil. Put the fish on the open, oiled fish grilling basket. Wash the lemons. Cut the lemons into thin slices and arrange on one side of the fish. Turn the trout over and arrange the lemons on the other side as well. Close the fish basket and grill the fish for about 15–20 minutes. Brush with oil throughout the cooking process and turn from time to time.

Serves 4. Preparation time: about 15 minutes

4 prepared trout

salt

freshly ground black pepper

2 cloves garlic

1 large fennel bulb

2 tablespoons fresh tarragon

2 untreated lemons

oil

Trout with almonds

4 freshly prepared trout

1 small zucchini

2 untreated lemons

1 bunch flat-leaved parsley

⅝ cup/5 oz/150 g butter

2 oz/60 g slivered (flaked)
   almonds

2 tablespoons oil

sea salt

Like all freshwater fish, trout has a particularly delicate flavor that should not be overpowered by the other ingredients. Almonds and fresh parsley beautifully complement the delicate taste of trout.

❶ Wash the trout briefly under the tap and pat dry with paper towels. Wash the lemons. Clean and wash the zucchini. Cut 1 lemon and the zucchini into slices and cut each slice into eight.

❷ Wash the parsley and pat dry with paper towels. Chop the parsley finely. Melt the butter and stir in the pieces of lemon, zucchini, parsley and slivered (flaked) almonds. Fill the trout with this mixture and secure if necessary with wooden cocktail sticks.

❸ Brush the skin with oil and season with salt. Put the trout in the fish grilling basket and grill over medium heat for about 5 minutes on each side. Cut the second lemon into slices and garnish the trout with them. Serve with rice and vegetables.

Serves 4. Preparation time: about 15 minutes

Trout with dill butter

4 fresh trout

salt

freshly ground mixed colored
  pepper

2 tablespoons dill

1 teaspoon lemon balm

1 teaspoon tarragon

4 tablespoons butter

4 teaspoons dry vermouth

oil

3 zucchini

1 onion

Dill has a particularly intense aroma that perfectly complements fish. In this recipe the trout is placed directly on the grid, so it is recommended that a sheet of foil should be put on the grid to prevent the cooking juices dropping into the fire.

❶ Wash the trout under running water, pat dry and season with salt and pepper inside and out.

❷ Knead the chopped dill, lemon balm and tarragon into the softened butter and vermouth. Fill the trout with the dill butter and brush the outside with oil.

❸ Wash the zucchini and cut in half lengthways. Peel and finely chop the onion finely and sprinkle over the zucchini. Season with salt and pepper and sprinkle with a little oil.

❹ Line the barbecue grid with foil. Put the trout on the grid with the opening upwards. Arrange the zucchini halves on the grid between the fish so that they are supported. Grill the fish and vegetables for about 10 minutes over medium heat. Arrange the trout with the zucchini halves on plates.

Serves 4. Preparation time: about 20 minutes

Herb-flavored herrings

A delicious aroma emerges from the fish parcels when they are opened. The herrings are cooked with plenty of herbs and garlic.

1 Wash the herrings under running water, wipe dry and season with salt and pepper. Peel the cloves of garlic and chop finely. Clean the scallions (spring onions) and chop into thin rings.

2 Wash the dill, chives and basil and pat dry with paper towels. Chop the dill, chives and basil very finely. Mix together the herbs, olive oil, garlic and scallions. Toss the fish in the herb mixture.

3 Oil 4 pieces of foil. Put a herring on each one and arrange the rest of the herb mixture on top of the herrings. Cut the lemon into 8 slices and garnish each fish with 2 slices of lemon. Seal the foil parcels and place in the fire and cook for about 10–15 minutes. Serve the herrings in the foil.

Serves 4. Preparation time: about 10 minutes

4 prepared herrings
sea salt
freshly ground white pepper
4 cloves garlic
4 scallions (spring onions)
½ bunch dill
½ bunch chives
½ bunch basil
4 tablespoons olive oil
1 large untreated lemon

Mackerel with gooseberries

Gooseberry sauce is a traditional accompaniment for mackerel in France. The combination of the fish and fruit may seem unusual at first glance, but the sophisticated flavor is really delicious.

1 Wash the mackerel and pat dry. Sprinkle the fish inside and out with the lemon juice and pepper. Brush the outside with olive oil.

2 Put the mackerel in fish grilling baskets and grill for about 6–8 minutes on each side, turning the baskets over several times.

3 Meanwhile, wash and prepare the gooseberries. Put in a pan with the sugar, sherry vinegar and butter. Cook for 2 or 3 minutes until the gooseberries are soft, stirring all the time. Wash the tarragon sprigs, shake dry, and chop the leaves finely. Remove the pan from the stove and stir the tarragon into the gooseberries. Serve the grilled mackerel with the hot gooseberry sauce.

Serves 6. Preparation time: about 15 minutes

6 prepared mackerel
2 tablespoons lemon juice
freshly ground black pepper
3 tablespoons olive-oil
9 oz/250 g gooseberries
2 teaspoons sugar
2 tablespoons sherry vinegar
2 tablespoons butter
2 sprigs tarragon

18 oz/500 g monkfish fillet

10 cherry tomatoes

1 clove garlic

2 tablespoons lemon juice

½ cup/4 fl oz/125 ml white wine

2 bay leaves

2 sprigs rosemary

3 tablespoons oil

freshly ground white pepper

Monkfish and tomato kebabs

A delicious starter for a barbecue meal that is quick and easy to prepare. The fish and tomatoes are marinated in a spicy sauce.

❶ Cut the fish fillets into pieces about 1½ in/4cm in size. Wash and cut the tomatoes in half and put the fish and tomatoes in a shallow dish.

❷ Peel and crush the garlic. Add to the lemon juice and white wine together with the bay leaves and a sprig of rosemary. Bring briefly to the boil. Let the mixture cool down and pour over the fish and tomatoes. Leave it marinate in the refrigerator for 1 hour.

❸ Remove the fish and tomatoes from the marinade and drain. Thread the fish and tomatoes alternately on oiled skewers. Cover the grid with foil and cook over medium heat for about 7 minutes, turning once. Season with freshly ground pepper.

Serves 4. Preparation time: about 25 minutes + 1 hour marinating

Salmon steaks in a mustard marinade

This dish is quick and easy to prepare. The addition of mustard, curry powder and capers adds a pleasantly spicy note to these juicy salmon steaks.

2 salmon steaks

1 teaspoon capers

juice of 1 lime

1 teaspoon curry powder

1 tablespoon strong mustard

1 tablespoon peanut (groundnut) oil

freshly ground mixed colored pepper

salt

❶ Wash the salmon steaks, pat dry with paper towels and put the salmon steaks in a shallow dish. Finely chop the capers and stir into the lime juice and peanut oil, together with the curry powder and strong mustard.

❷ Coat the salmon steaks on both sides with the marinade, cover, and leave in the refrigerator for 1 hour.

❸ Season the salmon steaks with freshly ground pepper and grill for about 3 minutes on each side. Season with salt only after the fish has been cooked. Serve with a mixed salad and white bread.

Serves 2. Preparation time: about 10 minutes + 1 hour marinating

Grilled sardines

They are a very popular dish in the Mediterranean, where grilled sardines are served in a variety ways. In Spain they are often served as a starter with a garlic mayonnaise and fresh bread. If fresh sardines cannot be found, frozen ones may be used.

18 medium sardines

juice of 2 lemons

freshly ground black pepper

2 cloves garlic

3 tablespoons chooped parsley

4 tablespoons oil

4 tablespoons breadcrumbs

❶ Wash the sardines, pat dry and season with lemon juice and pepper inside and out.

❷ Peel the cloves of garlic and chop finely. Add to the chopped parsley and stuff each sardine with this herb mixture.

❸ Brush the outside of the sardines with oil, coat in breadcrumbs and put them in the oiled fish grilling basket. Grill for about 2 minutes on each side.

Serves 6. Preparation time: about 20 minutes

Grilled salmon

Salmon is ideal for grilling because the flesh contains a fairly large amount of oil, which prevents it from drying out quickly. Salmon is particularly delicious brushed with melted butter, but it should not be placed too close to the fire because butter is burns very easily.

1 Wash the salmon cutlets and pat dry with paper towels. Place the salmon cutlets in a large dish and sprinkle with white wine and lemon juice. Season with freshly ground pepper and leave to stand for 10 minutes.

2 Melt the butter and brush onto both sides of the salmon cutlets. Put the cutlets in a large, rectangular fish grilling basket.

3 Put the tarragon, rosemary and savory on the charcoal. Put the grid as high as possible and place the fish grilling basket on top. Grill the salmon cutlets for about 3-4 minutes on each side, making sure that they do not burn.

4 Wash parsley, pat dry with paper towels and chop finely. Arrange the salmon cutlets on plates and sprinkle with chopped parsley. Serve with sauté potatoes.

Serves 6. Preparation time: about 20 minutes + 10 minutes marinating

6 salmon cutlets
2 tablespoons white wine
2 tablespoons lemon juice
freshly ground white pepper
⅝ cup/5 oz/100 g butter
1 sprig fresh tarragon
1 sprig fresh rosemary
1 sprig fresh savory
1 bunch smooth parsley

4 prepared whole fish of about
   1 lb/450 g each (such as
   snapper or herring)

2 tablespoons lemon juice

sea salt

freshly ground white pepper

1 bunch chervil

1 bunch lemon balm

4 tablespoons white wine

8 large white cabbage leaves

4 tablespoons oil

Whole fish in cabbage parcels

These grilled fish parcels are delicious. Wrapping the fish in white cabbage leaves preserves their delicate flavor, which is enhanced by their tasty herb filling.

❶ Wash the fish and wipe dry. Sprinkle with lemon juice inside and out. Season with salt and pepper.

❷ Wash chervil and lemon balm and pat dry with paper towels. Reserve a few chervil and lemon balm leaves for the garnish and chop the rest finely. Add the wine and stuff the fish with this mixture. Cook the cabbage leaves in boiling water for about 10–15 minutes. Remove and drain thoroughly.

❸ Place the stuffed fish on the cabbage leaves and wrap them up carefully. Brush 4 pieces of foil with oil, place the fish parcels on top and close the foil carefully. Put the parcels in the hot fire and cook for about 15 minutes. Remove the fish parcels from of the foil and arrange them on plates. Garnish with chervil and lemon balm.

Serves 4. Preparation time: about 30 minutes

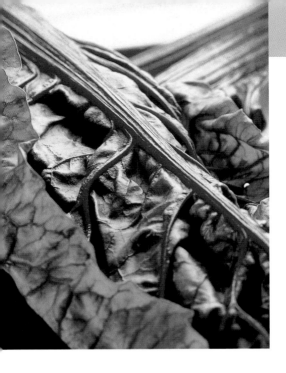

Tuna steaks in chard parcels

A sophisticated barbecue fish dish. The tuna fillets are first marinated in a spicy sauce and then wrapped in large chard leaves for grilling.

4 tuna fish steaks

1 leek

2 cloves garlic

1 teaspoon thyme

8 peppercorns

1 bay leaf

½ cup/4 fl oz/125 ml white wine

5 tablespoons oil

2 tablespoons lemon juice

8 large chard leaves

1 untreated lemon

❶ Wash the tuna steaks, pat dry and place in a shallow dish. Clean and wash the leeks. Cut in half lengthways, wash again and cut into thin strips. Peel and crush the garlic. Crush the thyme and pepper corns coarsely in a mortar.

❷ Add the leek, garlic, condiments and bay leaf to the white wine together with 4 tablespoons of oil and stir well. Pour over the fish and refrigerate covered for 1 hour.

❸ Pour this mixture into a large saucepan. Add 4½ cups/1¾ pints/1 litre of water, 1 tablespoon of oil and lemon juice and bring to the boil. Add the chard leaves, cover and blanch briefly until cooked but still firm to the bite. Then drain thoroughly.

❹ Remove the tuna steaks from the marinade and wrap each in 2 chard leaves. Wrap the tuna and chard parcels in foil and grill for about 15 minutes. Cut the lemon into slices. Remove the foil from the chard parcels and garnish with lemon slices.

Serves 4. Preparation time: about 35 minutes + 1 hour marinating

Mackerel brochettes

Grilled fish brochettes – on skewers – are a popular barbecue dish. Mackerel or other fish rich in oil should be used so that it does not dry out while being grilled.

1 Wash the fish and wipe them dry. Score the skin with a sharp knife 3 or 4 times on each side. Season the inside of each fish with pepper and lemon juice. Melt the butter and brush the inside of the fish with it.

2 Wash parsley, lovage and chervil and pat dry with paper towels. Chop the parsley, lovage and chervil finely and spoon inside the body cavity. Brush the outside of each fish with oil and sprinkle generously with herb salt.

3 Slide the mackerel onto large skewers and grill for about 10 minutes, turning several times. Serve with beer and pretzels.

Serves 4. Preparation time: about 20 minutes

4 prepared whole oily fish of about 1 lb/450 g each (such as mackerel, butterfish or pompano)

freshly ground mixed colored pepper

1 tablespoon lemon juice

4 tablespoons/2 oz/50 g butter

½ bunch parsley

¼ bunch lovage

½ bunch chervil

2 tablespoons oil

herb salt

Garlic shrimps

Shellfish at its finest! Fresh jumbo shrimps (prawns) in their shells are available from fresh fish counters. In this recipe they are coated with a garlic marinade and grilled.

1 Wash and dry the shrimps (scampi) and put in a shallow dish.

2 Peel and crush the cloves of garlic. Mix together with the marjoram, cayenne pepper, lemon juice and olive oil. Drain the anchovy fillets, chop finely and add to the marinade, stirring well to obtain a smooth mixture.

3 Pour the marinade over the scampi, cover and refrigerate for 1 hour. Line the grid with a sheet of foil. Put the scampi on the grid and cook over high heat for about 7 minutes, turning them several times.

Serves 6. Preparation time: about 20 minutes + 1 hour marinating

24 jumbo shrimps (prawns) in their shells

4 cloves garlic

1 teaspoon dried marjoram

1 pinch cayenne pepper

2 tablespoons lemon juice

2 tablespoons olive oil

2 preserved anchovy fillets

Char en papillote

Char are small freshwater fish of the trout family, and trout may also be used for this recipe. They are wrapped in waxed (greaseproof) paper or metal foil with fresh tomatoes and herbs, then grilled. The wrapping preserves the flavor of the individual ingredients and keeps the fish moist.

1 Wash the fish under running water and pat dry with paper towels. Sprinkle the fish inside and out with lemon juice and pepper.

2 Wash the tomatoes, remove the green stalks and cut into round slices. Wash the celery, clean and cut into fine rings. Wash the chervil, shake dry and chop the leaves finely.

3 Take 6 large sheets of waxed (greaseproof) paper or metal foil. Put a fish on each one. Surround with the tomato slices, celery and chervil. Sprinkle with lemon zest and pepper. Dot with flakes of butter

4 Wrap the fish in the paper and fold over to seal. Put a sheet of metal foil on the barbecue grid and place the fish parcels on it. Cook for about 30 minutes, turning carefully at the halfway stage. Serve the fish in their wrapping.

Serves 6. Preparation time: about 10 minutes

6 char or small trout

juice and peel of 2 untreated lemons

freshly ground white pepper

4 tomatoes

3 stalks celery

1 bunch chervil

4 tablespoons of butter

71

18 oz/500 g frozen peeled jumbo shrimps (prawns)

1 clove garlic

1 piece lemon grass

1 teaspoon finely grated ginger root

1 teaspoon turmeric

2 tablespoons lemon juice

4 tablespoons oil

4 tablespoons soy sauce

10 leaves basil

Jumbo shrimp kebabs with ginger

Frozen shrimps (prawns) are available in supermarkets. They can be turned into a real gourmet dish when seasoned with exotic, eastern spices as they are in this recipe.

❶ Put the frozen shrimps (prawns) in a shallow dish to thaw. Wash and pat dry. Peel and crush the cloves of garlic. Cut the lemon grass lengthways in half, remove the outer leaves and cut the inner white part into strips.

❷ Mix together the garlic, lemon grass, ginger and turmeric. Stir in the lemon juice, oil and soy sauce. Pour the marinade over the shrimps, cover and leave to stand in the refrigerator for 2 hours.

❸ Thread the shrimps on oiled skewers and grill over high heat for 7–10 minutes until glazed, turning several times. Chop the basil leaves finely and sprinkle over the hot kebabs.

Serves 4. Preparation time: about 20 minutes + 2 hours marinating

Barbecued lobster

This festive barbecue dish consists of lobster halves coated with herb butter. They are delicious eaten on their own, washed down with a bottle of good white wine and crisp French bread.

2 fresh boiled lobsters

2 cloves garlic

⅝ cup/5 oz/100 g butter

2 tablespoons lemon juice

chili powder

2 tablespoons chervil

1 tablespoon lemon balm

1 lemon

❶ Separate the claws at the joint by twisting them slightly. Place the lobster flat on a large board and cut in half lengthways from head to tail, using a large sharp knife. Crack open the claws and scoop out the flesh with a fork. Remove the intestine and gray sac from the head. Take out the roe and put to one side.

❷ Use the flesh from the claws and the roe to make the herb butter. Peel the cloves of garlic and chop finely. Add to the softened butter together with the lemon juice, chili powder, herbs, roe and lobster flesh. Mix together with a fork.

❸ Put half the herb butter on the lobster halves and place these on the grid with the cut sides up. Grill for about 10 minutes until the butter has melted. Wash and cut the lemon into eight. Garnish the lobster halves with the pieces of lemon and the rest of the herb butter.

Serves 4. Preparation time: about 25 minutes

Jumbo shrimps marinated in port wine

The sweet-and-sour marinade makes these jumbo shrimps (prawns) particularly delicious. When using a marinade containing acid ingredients such as lemon juice or vinegar, a glass or china dish should be used, rather than a metal one.

❶ Wash the jumbo shrimps (prawns), pat dry and put in a flat dish.

❷ Peal the shallots and chop finely. Mix in the vinegar, soy sauce, fish sauce, port wine, honey, curry powder and pepper to make the marinade.

❸ Pour the marinade over the shrimps. Cover the dish and leave in a cool place for 2 hours. Drain the shrimps well. Grill for about 3 minutes on each side. Garnish with fresh cilentro (coriander) leaves.

Serves 4–6. Preparation time: about 15 minutes + 2 hours marinating

Eel kebabs

This recipe is special pleasure for the palate. Eel is most commonly eaten smoked, but here fresh eel is combined with other strongly flavored ingredients and grilled.

❶ Skin the eels, wash, pat dry and cut into pieces about 1¼ in/3 cm long. Wash the parsley, shake dry and chop the leaves finely. Season the fish with sea salt and sprinkle each piece with chopped parsley.

❷ Wash and clean the zucchini. Cut into slices ¾ in/2 cm thick. Rub the oyster mushrooms with paper towels to clean and divide into bite-sized pieces. Cut the bell (sweet) pepper in half. Remove the stalk, seeds and white dividing membranes. Cut into wide strips. Wash and halve the tomatoes. Cut the smoked belly of pork into cubes of ¾ in/2 cm.

❸ Arrange the eel pieces alternately with vegetables, mushrooms, and pork on oiled metal skewers. Brush the kebabs with lemon juice and oil. Sprinkle with the paprika and pepper. Grill for about 5 minutes over high heat, turning from time to time. Serve garnished with parsley.

Serves 4. Preparation time: about 20 minutes

12 fresh jumbo shrimps (large prawns) in their shells

2 shallots

1 tablespoon white wine vinegar

3 tablespoons soy sauce

2 tablespoons Asian fish sauce

4 tablespoons port wine

1 tablespoon honey

1 teaspoon curry powder

chili powder

a few cilentro (coriander) leaves

1¼ lb/600 g prepared eels

1 bunch flat-leaved parsley

sea salt

1 zucchini

5 oz/150 g oyster mushrooms

1 red bell (sweet) pepper

5 cocktail-tomatoes

3½ oz/100 g smoked belly of pork

2 tablespoons of lemon juice

3 tablespoons vegetable oil

1 teaspoon paprika

freshly ground mixed colored pepper

4 rose fish fillets

sea salt

freshly ground black pepper

2 leeks

2 carrots

2 kohlrabi

2 tablespoons oil

2 tablespoons white wine

2 tablespoons cream

2 tablespoons chopped cress

Rose fish fillet on a bed of vegetables

Fish and vegetables – an unbeatable combination! This dish is quick and easy to make. All the ingredients are wrapped in foil and cooked on the barbecue until tender.

❶ Wash the rose fish fillets and wipe dry. Season with salt and pepper.

❷ Cut the leeks in half lengthways and wash well. Cut into pieces about ⅜ in/1 cm thick. Clean the carrots and grate coarsely. Peel the kohlrabi and cut into thin slices, then cut these into sticks.

❸ Stir the white wine, cream, and 1 tablespoon oil into the vegetables. Season with pepper. Oil 4 large pieces of foil and arrange the vegetables and fish on top. Sprinkle the fish with the rest of the oil.

❹ Salt the foil parcels and cook on the grill until ready. Open the parcels, arrange the fish on the vegetables, season with a little salt and pepper, and garnish with cress.

Serves 4. Preparation time: about 25 minutes

Fish kebabs

These delicate fish kebabs will appeal to everyone who likes Asian cooking, not least because of the sharp, spicy marinade in which the fish is prepared.

❶ Cut the fish fillets into pieces of about 1¼ in/3 cm and put in a flat dish. Mix the fish sauce with the fennel, cayenne pepper and lemon juice. Pour over the fish pieces.

❷ Peel the garlic and press it. Mix with the oil and put underneath the fish. Leave to stand for 30 minutes in a cool place.

❸ Wash and cut the limes into thin disks and alternate with the fish pieces on oiled wooden skewers. Grill over medium heat for about 7 minutes, turning several times and basting with the marinade. Serve the hot kebabs with white bread.

Serves 4. Preparation time: about 15 minutes + 30 minutes marinating

1¼ lb/600 g rose fish fillet
3 tablespoons Asian fish sauce
½ teaspoon turmeric
½ teaspoon fennel seeds
1 pinch cayenne pepper
3 tablespoons lemon juice
2 cloves garlic
2 tablespoons oil
2 limes
Oil for the wooden skewers

Cod fish kebabs with mango and mint

An exotic fish and fruit kebab, given a delightfully aromatic flavor by the fragrant mint. The mango must not be too ripe to be grilled, so check that the flesh is firm when buying.

1¼ lb/600 g cod fillets

1 bunch fresh mint

juice and grated zest of 2 untreated lemons

1 large mango

3 tablespoons oil

freshly ground black pepper

salt to taste

❶ Cut the cod fillets into pieces of about 1¼ in/3 cm and put in a flat dish. Wash mint and pat dry with paper towels. Take half the mint and chop it finely, then mix it with the lemon juice and grated lemon zest. Pour over the fish and leave to stand in a cool place for 30 minutes.

❷ Peel the mango and remove the pit (stone) from the flesh with a sharp knife. Cut into 1¼-in/3-cm pieces.

❸ Arrange the cubes of fish and mango on oiled skewers with a small leaf of mint between each piece. Paint the kebabs with oil and sprinkle with freshly ground pepper. Cover the barbecue with foil and cook for about 4 minutes, turning from time to time. Remove the skewers from the grill and add salt to taste.

Serves 4. Preparation time: about 25 minutes + 30 minutes marinating

Halibut fillet with dill

Halibut is fish high in fat with hardly any bones, which makes it ideal for barbecuing. Here it is covered with a herb paste that becomes crunchy when grilled.

❶ Wash the halibut fillets and pat dry. Mix the mayonnaise with crème fraîche and chili powder. Set aside some dill leaves to garnish. Finely chop the rest of the dill and the lovage and stir into the cream mixture.

❷ Mix the flour and ground almonds. Paint one side of the halibut fillets with the herb cream and sprinkle with the almond and flour mixture. Turn over and cover the other side in the same way.

❸ Cover the grill with foil and cook the fish fillets for 10–15 minutes. Garnish the fish with dill and serve with potato salad.

Serves 4. Preparation time: about 25 minutes

4 fillets of halibut

4 tablespoons mayonnaise

4 tablespoons crème fraîche

chili powder

4 sprigs fresh dill

some leaves of lovage

4 tablespoons spelt or wheat flour

2 tablespoons ground almonds

Fish rolls

Here fish and meat are combined in delicious little fish rolls stuffed with herbs and wrapped in ham, then grilled on the barbecue. Serve a strongly-flavored white wine with them.

❶ Wash the fish fillets and pat dry. Put the fish on a surface with the skinned side down and sprinkle with lemon juice and pepper. Scatter the grated cheese over them.

❷ Wash the chives, shake dry and cut into small cylinders. Wash the dill, shake dry and finely chop. Sprinkle the herbs over the fish fillets. Roll up each fillet with the herbs inside, wrap with a slice of ham and secure with a wooden toothpick or thin skewer.

❸ Brush the fish rolls with oil, put metal foil on the grid and cook for about 15 minutes at medium heat.

Serves 4. Preparation time: about 10 minutes

4 fresh plaice fillets

2 tablespoons lemon juice

freshly ground black pepper

2 tablespoons grated Emmental or other hard cheese

1 bunch chive

1 bunch dill

4 slices lean cooked ham

2 tablespoons vegetable oil

Vegetables

Vegetables cooked in the embers

This is a beautiful, colorful combination of vegetables that can be varied according to taste and what is available on the market. For instance, the celery can be replaced by fennel and the zucchini by carrots. These vegetable kebabs are delicious served with baked potatoes and as an accompaniment to grilled fish.

1 eggplant (aubergine)

2 slices cheese, ³⁄₁₆ in/5 mm thick

4 tablespoons/2 oz/50 g butter

2 roots celeriac

½ teaspoon paprika

½ teaspoon garlic salt

4 large tomatoes

4 tablespoons/2 oz/50 g crème fraîche

1 zucchini

salt

½ teaspoon cayenne pepper

1 Wash the eggplant (aubergine), remove the stalk and cut into slices ⅜ in/1 cm thick. Cut the slices of cheese into pieces about ¾ in/2 cm square and place one between every two slices of eggplant. Season with salt and pepper and dot with a few flakes of butter.

2 Wash the celeriac, peel and cut each one into eight pieces. Season with paprika and garlic salt. Dot the rest of the butter on the pieces of celeriac.

3 Wash the tomatoes, cut in half and coat with crème fraîche.

4 Wash the zucchini, cut off the ends and cut into slices.

5 Arrange the vegetables on 4 pieces of foil and sprinkle with cayenne pepper. Wrap into parcels. Cook the parcels in the embers for 10–15 minutes.

Serves 4. Preparation time: about 20 minutes

Spicy potato kebabs

The attraction of these kebabs lies in the spices that immediately evoke Indian cuisine. The cardamom used in this recipe is a member of the ginger family and is native to southern India. It is one of the most ancient spices in the world.

1 Peel the potatoes and boil in salted water for about 10–15 minutes. They should not be completely cooked through. Remove from the water and leave to cool. Thread 4 potatoes on each skewer.

2 Stir together the mango chutney, oil, tomato paste, curry powder, cardamom and yogurt.

3 Coat the potato kebabs all over with this mixture.

4 Cook on the barbecue grid over high heat for about 10 minutes, turning several times.

5 Garnish with parsley.

Serves 4–6. Preparation time: about 35 minutes

18 oz/500 g small waxy potatoes

salt

12 teaspoons strong mango chutney

6 tablespoons peanut (groundnut) oil

2 teaspoons tomato paste

1 teaspoon curry powder

1 teaspoon ground cardamom

2 tablespoons yogurt

parsley as garnish

Garlic barbecued in foil

This is a more intensely flavored variation on garlic butter. When the garlic is ready, the flesh will have softened to a paste. It is pressed out the skins with a knife and spread on slices of white bread or served with grilled fish or meat.

1 Remove the outer skin of the garlic bulb. Cut 4 squares of foil and brush generously with oil. Put one bulb on each piece of foil. Pour olive oil over it and season with salt and pepper.

2 Fold the foil to make parcels and cook on the edge of the barbecue grid for about 25 minutes.

Serves 4. Preparation time: about 5 minutes

4 bulbs garlic

4 tablespoons olive oil

salt

freshly ground black pepper

Potato chips (crisps)

Potato chips (crisps) are always a popular and welcome snack and they can be bought in all kinds of flavors. But home-made ones are much nicer than bought ones and contain less fat. They can be seasoned to taste with garlic salt, paprika or curry powder.

salt

2–3 large potatoes

4–6 tablespoons vegetable oil

❶ Bring a saucepan of salted water to the boil.

❷ Peel the potatoes and cut lengthways into very thin slices.

❸ Immediately put the slices in hot water and stir well so that thy do not stick to each other. Leave them in the water for 3-4 minutes until they have become malleable.

❹ Remove the potato slices from the water and drain well. Roll them up and place 5 or 6 rolls ⅜ in/1 cm apart on each skewer.

❺ Brush with oil and cook on a hot grid for about 10–15 minutes, turning several times.

❻ Drain briefly just before serving.

Serves 4–6. Preparation time: about 20 minutes

Barbecued onions

When cooked, braised or grilled, onions lose their sharp taste and acquire a sweeter one, become a delicious vegetable. They are excellent served with meat or fish.

❶ Peel the onions and cut into slices ⅜ in/1 cm thick. Do not let the onion rings separate. Season with herb salt.

❷ Beat the cream until semi-stiff and spread on one side of the onion slices. Crush the peppercorns in a mortar and sprinkle over the onions.

❸ Put the slices of onion in a grill basket on the grid, coated side up. Grill for 5–8 minutes.

❹ When the onions are about to turn black, sprinkle a few flakes of butter on top.

❺ Arrange on a plate with the peppery side upwards. Garnish with sprigs of thyme and serve.

Serves 4–6. Preparation time: about 10 minutes

2 large red onions
herb salt
3½ oz/100 g cream
1 tablespoon black peppercorns
butter
sprigs of thyme as garnish

Baked potatoes

This simple recipe can be varied to taste by changing the ingredients of the sauce. The bacon or ham can be bought ready diced in most supermarkets, making this recipe even easier.

8 medium floury potatoes

2 tablespoons olive oil

1 teaspoon sweet ground paprika

3–4 drops Tabasco

5 oz/150 g curd cheese

½ cup/4 fl oz/125 ml cream

1 teaspoon mustard

juice of 1 lemon

salt

freshly ground white pepper

5 oz/150 g diced bacon or ham

1 tablespoon butter

❶ Wash the potatoes under the tap and scrub clean.

❷ Cut 8 pieces of foil, one for each potato.

❸ Stir the Tabasco and paprika into the olive oil and brush the foil with it. Wrap the potatoes in the foil and cook in the embers for about 40 minutes.

❹ Stir together the cheese, cream, mustard and lemon juice to make a smooth sauce and season with salt and pepper.

❺ Cook the diced bacon or ham in a skillet (frying pan) with a little butter until crisp. Pour the sauce over the potatoes and spoon on the diced bacon or ham.

Serves 4. Preparation time: about 15 minutes

Zucchini in herb marinade

An easy recipe that is quick to prepare and yet very sophisticated. It is important to baste the zucchini often while they are being grilled because they tend to dry out quickly otherwise. This dish can be served with grilled fish or meat but it is also delicious with a fresh herb dip as a vegetarian dish.

8–10 medium, firm zucchini

4–5 leaves basil

4–5 fresh leaves mint

1 teaspoon thyme

2 tablespoons dry white wine

2 tablespoons lemon juice

4 tablespoons olive oil

salt

❶ Wash, clean and prepare the zucchini. Score the skin all round with a sharp, pointed knife so that the marinade can penetrate into the flesh.

❷ Chop all the herbs finely, transfer to a shallow dish and stir in the wine, lemon juice, olive oil and salt.

❸ Put the zucchini in this marinade and turn over so that they absorb the marinade on all sides. Cover and stand for about 10 minutes.

❹ Cook over a high heat for 8–10 minutes until they are cooked but still firm. Continue basting the zucchini with the marinade while they are cooking.

Serves 4. Preparation time: about 10 minutes + 10 minutes marinating

Bell (sweet) peppers with potato and egg

With its potato and egg filling, this recipe is rich in carbohydrates and protein, while bell (sweet) peppers are rich in vitamin C. It therefore make a healthy vegetarian meal. The mayonnaise can be replaced with sour cream to make the filling lighter.

❶ Wash the peppers. Remove the top and the seeds to make little "containers".

❷ Shell the eggs. Peel the potatoes. Cut the eggs and the potatoes into small dice. Peel the onions and chop finely.

❸ Stir the mayonnaise or sour cream and mustard into the potato, egg and onion mixture and season with paprika, salt and pepper.

❹ Spoon the filling into the peppers and wrap each one in a piece of foil.

❺ Cook the peppers for 30 minutes on the grid or directly in the embers until soft.

Serves 4. Preparation time: about 45 minutes

4 red bell (sweet) peppers

4 hard-cooked (hard-boiled) eggs

4–6 cooked potatoes

1 small onion

3 tablespoons mayonnaise or sour cream

2 teaspoons strong mustard

1 teaspoon paprika

½ teaspoon garlic salt

freshly ground black pepper

oil for the foil

Stuffed vine leaves

Melted cheese in vine leaves is certainly not a common barbecue dish, but this is a simple recipe with a very delicate flavor, making it an interesting variation on the traditional dish of vine leaves stuffed with rice. Packs of vine leaves can be found in Greek or Turkish stores.

14 oz/400 g soft goat's cheese

freshly ground black pepper

2 tablespoons chopped herbs

20 preserved vine leaves

olive oil

white bread

❶ Cut the cheese into thick cubes, season with pepper and stir in the chopped herbs.

❷ Wash the vine leaves and drain thoroughly. Then spread them out and place the cubes of cheese in the middle of the vine leaves. Fold down the vine leaf on all four sides to make a tidy parcel.

❸ Brush 4 large pieces of foil with olive oil and wrap 5 vine leaf parcels in each piece of foil.

❹ Put the aluminum parcels directly in the embers for a good 10 minutes.

❺ Remove the foil. Put the vine leaves on plates and cut them open so that the cheese flows out . Serve with white bread.

Serves 4. Preparation time: about 10 minutes

8 medium tomatoes

8 tablespoons dry red wine

salt

freshly ground black pepper

salad leaves or parsley as garnish

Grilled tomatoes

The tomatoes used in this recipe should be very firm and not too small. The dish is delicious served with grilled steak or hamburger. Because the cooking time is similar to that needed by meat, they can be grilled on the barbecue at the same time.

❶ Put each tomato on a piece of foil. Press the foil all round the tomato, leaving just a small opening at the top but not allowing juices to escape. at the bottom

❷ Pour 1 tablespoon of red wine over each tomato. Season with salt and pepper.

❸ Grill the tomatoes over medium heat (at the edge of the grid) for 10–15 minutes.

❹ Remove the foil carefully, reserving the wine and tomato juices. Arrange the tomatoes on a plate. Pour the wine sauce over the tomatoes. Wash the salad leaves or parsley, chop and garnish the tomatoes.

Serves 4. Preparation time: about 5 minutes

Stuffed eggplants (aubergines)

The smooth, shiny purple skin of the eggplant (aubergine) is particularly attractive and it is an ideal vegetable for stuffing. This recipe uses the eggplant's flesh combined with tomatoes and herbs.

❶ Cut off a lengthways slice from each eggplant. These will later be used as lids.

❷ Spoon the flesh out of the eggplant, leaving a layer inside about ⅜ in/1 cm thick. Cut the flesh into small dice.

❸ Peel the onion and garlic, chop finely and sauté in a little butter in a saucepan. Add the diced eggplant and cook gently until done. Remove from the heat.

❹ Wash the tomatoes, pour hot water over them and puree in a blender. Add to the eggplant mixture together with breadcrumbs, Parmesan cheese and thyme and stir well.

❺ Spoon the filling into the hollowed-out eggplants, put the "lids" back on and wrap in oiled foil.

❻ Grill on the grid or directly in the embers for 20–30 minutes until the eggplant has softened but still has some bite. Garnish with sprigs of thyme.

Serves 4. Preparation time: about 35 minutes

4 eggplants (aubergines)

1 onion

1 clove garlic

1½ tablespoons/¾ oz/20 g butter

7 oz/200 g fresh tomatoes

1 cup/2 oz/50 g breadcrumbs

½ cup/2 oz/50 g grated Parmesan cheese

1 teaspoon dried thyme

salt

freshly ground black pepper

sprigs of thyme to garnish

oil for the foil

Stuffed tomatoes

In this recipe the tomatoes form small "containers" for the filling but they also add taste and fragrance to the dish. This is why the quality of the tomatoes is very important. Where possible, always choose tomatoes that have ripened in the sun rather than those produced in greenhouses.

8 ripe beef tomatoes

18 oz/500 g spinach

1 white onion

1 tablespoon butter

3 tablespoons olive oil

salt

black pepper

9 oz/250 g diced bacon or ham

3 tablespoons breadcrumbs

3 tablespoons grated Parmesan cheese

❶ Wash the tomatoes, cut off the tops and scoop out the flesh. Cut the flesh and the top into cubes.

❷ Carefully wash the spinach several times. Peel the onion, cut into cubes and sauté gently in a saucepan in some olive oil. Add the spinach and cook gently for about 5 minutes. Season with salt and pepper.

❸ Sauté the diced bacon or ham in a skillet (frying pan) with 1 tablespoon oil until crisp.

❹ Mix together the diced tomatoes, spinach, onion and bacon. Add the breadcrumbs and Parmesan cheese.

❺ Spoon this mixture into the hollowed-out tomatoes.

❻ Wrap the stuffed tomatoes in foil and grill for about 10–15 minutes.

Serves 4. Preparation time: about 30 minutes

Stuffed mushrooms

White mushrooms are preferable to brown ones for this recipe because mushrooms tend to go darker when cooked on the barbecue and look less appealing. There are many variations on this recipe. For a vegetarian version, just leave out the ham.

❶ Gently detach the mushroom stalks by twisting lightly. Carefully clean the mushrooms and pat dry.

❷ Peel the onion and garlic cloves. Finely chop them and the parsley, then mix together with the ham.

❸ Add the olive oil and season with salt and pepper.

❹ Spoon the mixture onto the mushrooms and sprinkle with Parmesan cheese. Prepare 12 pieces of foil large enough to wrap the mushrooms and brush with oil. Put one stuffed mushroom on each piece of foil and make a parcel. Put on the grid of the barbecue and cook for 10–15 minutes. The mushrooms are ready when the Parmesan cheese has melted to a beautiful golden brown colour.

Serves 4–6. Preparation time: about 25 minutes

12 large mushrooms

1 onion

2 cloves garlic

1 bunch parsley

3½ oz/100 g cooked ham, cut into fine strips

2 tablespoons olive oil

salt

freshly ground black pepper

½ cup/2 oz/50 g grated Parmesan cheese

Mushrooms in bacon parcels

20 firm mushrooms

⅝ cup/5 oz/100 g butter

2 tablespoons lemon juice

3 tablespoons chopped parsley

10 slices bacon without rind

freshly ground black pepper

Use large mushrooms that are easy to thread on a skewer and wrap in bacon. As an alternative, the mushrooms can be replaced with pitted (stoned) dates. They are just as easy to prepare and also taste delicious.

❶ Cook the mushrooms for 1 minute in boiling water, remove and drain well.

❷ Melt the butter and stir in the lemon juice, pepper and chopped parsley.

❸ Cut the bacon slices in half and wrap each half slice round a mushroom. Then thread 5 wrapped mushrooms on each skewer.

❹ Coat the bacon-wrapped mushrooms with the parsley butter and grill for 3–5 minutes over medium heat until the bacon is beautifully crisp. Sprinkle with freshly ground pepper.

Serves 4. Preparation time: 20 minutes

Grilled oyster mushrooms

Oyster mushrooms are so named because of the similarity in colour with the shellfish. The juicy flesh of the oyster mushroom is ideally suited to grilling and baking.

1 Wash the oyster mushrooms under running water and wipe dry with paper towels.

2 Peel the cloves of garlic, crush and add to the softened butter, olive oil and lemon juice. Add the chopped mint and season with salt and pepper.

3 Brush the marinade on both sides of the mushrooms and grill on the barbecue for about 2–3 minutes on each side.

Serves 4. Preparation time: about 15 minutes

18 oz/500 g oyster mushrooms
3 cloves garlic
juice of 1 lemon
5 tablespoons olive oil
2 tablespoons/1 oz/25 g butter
1 sprig fresh mint
salt
freshly ground black pepper

Grilled prunes and bacon

Only a few ingredients are required for this favorite American recipe and very little work is involved, making it an excellent barbecue dish.

Wrap each prune in a slice of bacon and secure with a toothpick. Grill until the bacon is crisp, turning from time to time.

Serves 4. Preparation time: about 3 minutes

16 prunes
16 slices lean bacon

4 fresh corncobs (or canned)

salt

oil or unsalted butter for cooking

pepper

4 tablespoons/2 oz/50 g unsalted butter

2 tablespoons fresh green peppercorns

1 dash brandy

Barbecued corncobs

Corncobs are particularly popular with children because they can be eaten without a knife and fork. But adults also enjoy them as a welcome change, especially this rather refined recipe.

❶ Pre-cook the fresh corncobs in salted water for about 15 minutes and wipe dry. If using canned or bottled corncobs, drain them thoroughly.

❷ Coat the corncobs with oil or softened butter and grill on all sides for about 10 minutes. When cooked, sprinkle with salt and pepper.

❸ Beat the butter until foamy and stir in the crushed pepper corns. Season with a dash of cognac and serve as a sauce with the corncob.

Serves 4. Preparation time: about 20 minutes

2 large, firm zucchini

1 leek

1 red bell (sweet) pepper

1 tomato

3½ oz/100 g cooked green lentils

a few small basil leaves

salt

freshly ground black pepper

2 tablespoons toasted pine
   kernels or chopped walnuts

Zucchini with green lentils

Zucchinis are excellent vegetables for the barbecue, and their shape makes them perfect for stuffing with every kind of filling. Best known is the rice and ground (minced) meat filling, but here is an interesting meatless variation using lentils and vegetables that is delicious.

❶ Wash and clean the zucchini. Cut in half lengthways and scoop out the flesh with a teaspoon. Put the flesh in a bowl.

❷ Wash the leek well and cut into rings. Wash and finely chop the bell (sweet) pepper and tomato. Mix together the leek, tomato, zucchini flesh, lentils and basil in a bowl. Season with salt and pepper to taste and spoon into the hollowed-out zucchini.

❸ Wrap each zucchini half in 2 pieces of metal foil. Leave some air space above the filling so that the steam can circulate. Grill the zucchini for about 20 minutes.

❹ Remove the foil from the zucchini halves and sprinkle with toasted pine kernels or chopped walnuts.

Serves 4. Preparation time: about 15 minutes

Vegetable kebabs

A quick and easy recipe that can be varied to taste. The only require-
ment is that the vegetables are suitable for threading on skewers. These
vegetable kebabs can be served with potatoes or as an accompaniment
for grilled meat or fish. They are delicious with a spicy tomato sauce.

1 Peel the carrots and cut them into slices. Wash the corncobs and slice them.
Wash the cauliflower and separate into florets. Peel the onions.

2 Cook the various vegetables separately, except for the tomatoes. They should
be firm to the bite.

3 Drain the vegetables and arrange them in separate piles. Prepare 10 skewers.

4 Thread the vegetables evenly onto the skewers and brush with some oil. Grill
for 5–10 minutes, turning regularly. Serve with a variety of sauces or dips.

Serves 4–6. Preparation time: about 35 minutes

4 large carrots

3 small corncobs

1 cauliflower

9 oz/250 g cocktail onions

12 cherry tomatoes

chili oil

Mixed vegetable kebabs

This is a perfect vegetarian alternative to meat kebabs. They can be made with any kind of vegetable depending on the season and are always a visual treat. There are endless possibilities in the choice and composition of these vegetable kebabs.

1 Cook the shallots, unpeeled, in boiling water for about 15 minutes. Remove from the water and peel immediately.

2 Wash the peppers, tomatoes and mushrooms. Cut each pepper into four and remove the seeds. Wash and prepare the mushrooms, then pat dry with paper towels.

3 Cook the broccoli for 3 minutes, and the cauliflower for 10 minutes in boiling salted water. Remove from the water and leave to cool.

4 Oil 12 long wooden skewers with walnut oil. Thread the vegetables on the skewers in a repeating sequence. Grill over medium heat for 15–20 minutes, turning several times. Finally, season with salt and pepper.

Serves 3–4. Preparation time: about 40 minutes

5 oz/150 g shallots

1 yellow and 1 red bell (sweet) pepper

7 oz/200 g cherry tomatoes

5 oz/150 g medium, firm mushrooms

walnut oil

5 oz/150 g broccoli or cauliflower

herb salt

freshly ground black pepper

14 oz/400 g soft bean curd (tofu)

1 leek

1 carrot

5 oz/150 g soy bean sprouts

Bean curd (tofu) with vegetables

Bean curd or tofu is a food of cheese-like texture made from the yellow soy beans. It is very rich in protein, easy to digest, low in calories, and cholesterol free, characteristics that make it the perfect substitute for meat. Tofu is firm enough to be sliced and fried, braised or grilled. Because of its rather neutral taste, it is best served with a variety of dips and marinades.

❶ Cut the bean curd (tofu) into slices and soak in a marinade, chosen for instance from the section on Marinades, Sauces and Dips, for 1 hour.

❷ Clean and wash the leek. Rinse the sprouts in a sieve and strain. Wash and peel the carrot. Cut the leeks into rings and the carrots into slices and stir into the bean sprouts.

❸ Arrange the vegetables on four pieces of foil, add the bean curd slices and close the parcel.

❹ Grill on the edge of the grid over medium heat for about 15 minutes.

Serves 4. Preparation time: about 15 minutes + 1 hour marinating

Marinated cheese kebabs

A delicious, nourishing dish that is also popular with vegetarians. The combination of cheese with fresh vegetables and herbs makes it easier to digest. The recipe can be varied by replacing the peppers with broccoli and the mushrooms with tomatoes. These kebabs are delicious served with a spicy tomato sauce and potatoes.

❶ Cut the bell (sweet) peppers in half, remove the seeds and white pith, then wash. Peel the onions. Clean the mushrooms with paper towels. Cut the peppers, onions and cheese into large pieces of roughly similar size. Peel the garlic and chop finely.

❷ Wash and dry the mint, chives and cress. Chop finely. Mix these with the thyme, oregano, lemon juice, olive oil and pepper to make the marinade.

❸ Put the pieces of cheese, pepper and onions with the mushrooms in a bowl. Pour the marinade over all and refrigerate for 24 hours.

❹ Thread the pieces of cheese, vegetables and onion on a metal skewer and grill on the barbecue for 10 minutes. Baste with the remainder of the marinade, turning the skewers from time to time.

Serves 4. Preparation time: about 20 minutes + 24 hours marinating

2 green bell (sweet) peppers

2 onions

1½ lb/700 g cheese, such as Emmenthal or Camembert

1 clove garlic

2 teaspoons mint

2 teaspoons thyme

2 teaspoons oregano

2 teaspoons chopped chives

2 teaspoons chopped cress

juice of 1 lemon

½ cup/3½ fl oz/100 ml olive oil

freshly ground mixed colored pepper

8 mushrooms

Cheese and vegetable parcels

This recipe can be made with processed cheese or hard cheese that melts easily. The choice of vegetables is also unlimited. For instance, the zucchini and eggplant (aubergines) could be replaced with broccoli and carrots.

2 beef tomatoes

1 zucchini

1 eggplant (aubergine)

1 yellow bell (sweet) pepper

7 oz/200 g thin slices processed cheese or hard cheese such as Gruyère or Emmenthal

freshly ground mixed colored pepper

❶ Wash the vegetables. Remove the stalks from the tomatoes and cut each into eight pieces. Cut off the ends of the zucchini and eggplant (aubergine) and cut into thin slices. Cut the peppers in half, remove the stalk, white skin and seeds, and cut into strips.

❷ Brush oil on 4 pieces of foil. Arrange similar amounts of vegetables on each one. Season generously with pepper and place the cheese slices on top. Seal the parcels and grill for about 15 minutes over medium heat.

Serves 4. Preparation time: about 10 minutes

Barbecued cheese sandwiches

Cheese is ideal for cooking on the barbecue. Processed cheeses are suitable, as are hard cheeses such as Gruyère, Emmenthal or Gouda. These sandwiches make a delicious snack, served with beer or red wine.

7 oz/200 g processed cheese, Gruyère or Gouda

2 tomatoes

8 slices of bread or baguette

softened butter

chili powder

paprika

❶ Cut the cheese into slices. Wash the tomatoes, remove the stalks and cut into slices. Butter all the slices of bread on both sides and put 4 of them on 4 pieces of foil.

❷ Arrange the sliced tomatoes on the 4 slices of bread and add the cheese slices. Season with salt, chili powder and paprika.

❸ Put the other slices of bread on top and wrap in the foil.

❹ Grill the parcels over high heat for about 6–8 minutes.

Serves 4. Preparation time: about 10 minutes

Grilled polenta slices with garlic butter and tomato sauce

When cooking the slices on the barbecue grid, a useful trick is to rotate the slices about 30 degrees after 2 minutes, which creates a decorative diamond-shaped pattern on them.

1 cup/8 fl oz/250 ml milk

1 cup/8 fl oz/250 ml broth (stock)

6 tablespoons/3 oz/75 g garlic
    butter

salt

freshly grated nutmeg

5 oz/150 g cornmeal, semolina or
    farina

1 egg

1 egg yolk

2 cloves garlic

1 sprig rosemary

1 chilli pod

3 tablespoons olive-oil

18 oz/500 g tomatoes

❶ To make the polenta slices, put the milk, broth (stock) and 2 tablespoons of garlic butter in a small pan and bring to boil. Flavor generously with salt and nutmeg.

❷ Pour the cornmeal, semolina or farina into the pan while stirring vigorously. Continue stirring until the polenta starts to bind. Cover and simmer on the lowest heat for 40 minutes, stirring from time to time. Next stir the egg andthen the egg yolk one after the other into the mass while it is still hot.

❸ Pour the polenta onto an oiled metal sheet in a layer about ⅜ in/1 cm thick and leave to cool.

❹ For the sauce, peel the garlic, wash the rosemary, pat dry, and remove the needles from the stem. Wash the chilli pod, cut open lengthways, remove the seeds and chop the pod finely. Heat the olive oil in a pan and lightly brown the garlic and chilli pod with the rosemary needles.

❺ Meanwhile wash the tomatoes and remove the stalks. Chop the tomatoes into large dice and add to the pan. Add salt to taste and cook on a medium heat for about 10 minutes.

❻ Cut the polenta into slices. Oil the grid well and grill the slices on both sides for about 3–4 minutes. When the polenta slices are ready, cut the garlic butter in pieces and spread it on them. Serve with the tomato sauce.

Serves 4. Preparation time: about 60 minutes

Zucchini and onions

A very simple dish, with the ham giving the vegetables a delicious flavor. It can be modified at will, so this recipe could be varied for instance by using broccoli or carrots. Tomato salsa or barbecue sauce make an excellent accompanying relish.

❶ Peel the onions and cut into rings. Wash the zucchini and cut into slices.

❷ Mix the vegetables together and season generously with salt and pepper.

❸ Cut the cooked ham into slices and stir into the vegetables with the oil.

❹ Divide the vegetable mixture into 4 servings and wrap each one in foil.

❺ Cook the foil parcels on the grill for 10 minutes. Then unwrap them and serve immediately while they are still hot.

Serves 4. Preparation time: about 10 minutes

2 onions
2 zucchini
salt
freshly ground black pepper
5 oz/150 g cooked ham
1 tablespoon sunflower oil

Buttermilk potatoes

The potato is one of the world's greatest basic foods. Contrary to popular opinion, it is no more fattening than a lean steak, for instance. It is the ingredients that make this nutritious dish so delicious.

❶ Wash and scrub the potatoes well in running water and pat dry with paper towels. Wrap each one in a square of foil and put in the embers of the barbecue for 1 to 1½ hours.

❷ Peel the onion, chop finely and fry in a pan with the diced bacon until golden.

❸ Mix the buttermilk and crème fraîche together, adding salt and pepper to taste. Then stir it into the onion and bacon mixture.

❹ Serve the mixture with the hot potatoes and garnish with the cress.

Serves 4. Preparation time: about 5 minutes

4 large potatoes
1 onion
3½ oz/100 g diced bacon
⅞ cup/7 fl oz/200 ml buttermilk
1 cup/8 fl oz/250 ml crème
  fraîche
salt
freshly ground mixed colored
  pepper
chopped cress as garnish

Cheese-stuffed bell (sweet) peppers

These large peppers with a soft cheese filling are delicious and easily prepared. They are excellent served with barbecued meat or sausages, or simply with white bread.

8 long green bell (sweet) peppers

14 oz/400 g low-fat soft cheese (quark)

3½ oz/100 g grated Gouda or other hard cheese

4 tablespoons olive oil

16 black pitted olives

6–8 leaves basil

1 clove garlic

salt

freshly ground black pepper

❶ Wash the peppers. Remove the stalk and cut in half lengthways. Remove the fibre and seeds.

❷ Mix the soft cheese with the grated cheese and olive oil. Finely chop the olives, basil and garlic, then stir into the cheese mixture. Add salt and pepper.

❸ Fill the half-peppers with the mixture.

❹ Grill over strong heat for about 20 minutes.

Serves 4–6. Preparation time: about 10 minutes

Sweet-and-sour eggplants (aubergines)

The eggplant or aubergine is inedible raw and does not have a particularly strong flavor in itself, so it is often spiced. This sweet-and-sour variation goes very well with barbecued steaks or cutlets.

❶ Wash, prepare and peel the eggplants (aubergines) and cut into quarters, then cut into bite-sized cubes.

❷ Peel the clove of garlic, crush with a garlic press and mix with the oil, vinegar, mustard, sugar, herbs and pepper.

❸ Mix the eggplant in the marinade and leave for 15 minutes, stirring occasionally.

❹ Put the cubes on skewers and grill over high heat for 15 minutes, turning them several times.

Serves 4. Preparation time: about 10 minutes + 15 minutes marinating

2 medium eggplants (aubergines)
1 clove garlic
4 tablespoons olive oil
3 tablespoons balsamic vinegar
½ teaspoon strong mustard
1 tablespoon chopped lovage
1 teaspoon oregano
pepper
1 tablespoon sugar

Grilled tomatoes with peanut cream

Tomatoes are often cooked on the barbecue, but they are not very filling. With the high-protein peanut cream this is a more substantial dish.

❶ Wash the tomatoes and cut a cross in the stalk end with a pointed knife.

❷ Crush the cloves of garlic and mix with 3 tablespoons of olive oil and oregano. Spread on the tomatoes, wrap in metal foil and grill for 10 minutes.

❸ Heat the remaining olive oil in a pan. Peel the onions, chop finely and cook in the oil until transparent. Add half the peanuts and cook until they start to color.

❹ Add a little water and puree in the blender until smooth. Roughly chop the rest of the peanuts and stir into the puree. Season to taste with pepper and soy sauce. Serve with the grilled tomatoes.

Serves 4. Preparation time: about 15 minutes

8 large beef tomatoes
1 cloves of garlic
6 tablespoons of olive-oil
1 teaspoons of oregano
4 small onions
1 cup/5 oz/150 g shelled peanuts
freshly ground black pepper
soy-sauce

113

Desserts

Walnut toffee and bananas

½ cup/2 oz/50 g walnut pieces

⅓ cup/2 oz/60 g brown sugar

6 firm bananas

4 tablespoons/2 oz/50 g butter

9 oz/250 g vanilla ice cream

This unusual barbecue dessert will be had to resist – bananas with home-made walnut toffee and vanilla ice-cream!

❶ Chop the walnut pieces finely and put in a small non-stick pan with the sugar. Heat gently, stirring continuously until the sugar has melted and acquired a syrupy consistency.

❷ Line a large baking pan with waxed (greaseproof) paper and pour the hot syrup over it. Leave the syrup to cool down. As soon as it has set, break it into pieces with a knife.

❸ Peel the bananas and cut them in half lengthways. Cover the bottom of a large aluminum foil tray with flakes of butter. Arrange the banana halves in it and sprinkle with the crushed walnut toffee. Carefully cover with foil and grill over medium heat for about 8–10 minutes. Arrange the hot toffee bananas on plates with a scoop of vanilla ice-cream on each one.

Serves 6. Preparation time: about 15 minutes

Fruit flambé

Brandy is poured over the hot grilled fruit and ignited in front of the guests – this is great fun to watch and also very delicious! But take great care when doing it.

❶ Cut the peaches in half and remove the pits (stones). Peel them and cut the flesh into eight segments. Peel the bananas and cut into thick slices. Peel the pears, cut in half, core and cut into segments. Clean the raspberries.

❷ Heat 1 tablespoon of butter with the honey and powdered cinnamon. Grease a large foil tray with the rest of the butter. Arrange the segments of fruit in the tray and pour the honey and butter mixture over them. Grill for about 7 minutes over medium heat, stirring the fruit several times.

❸ Heat the brandy in a pan until it is warm – not hot. Remove it from the heat. Arrange the hot fruit on the plates. Pour the brandy over the fruit. Keeping spectators at a distance and turning the face away, set light to the brandy with a long match. Serve immediately.

Serves 4–6. Preparation time: about 15 minutes

2 peaches

2 bananas

2 pears

7 oz/200 g raspberries

2 tablespoons butter

2 teaspoons honey

1 teaspoon powdered cinnamon

½ cup/4 fl oz/125 ml brandy

Bananas with ham

Sweet and savory flavors are combined in this delicious alliance of bananas and ham.

❶ Peel the bananas and cut in half lengthways. Cut each pineapple slice into eight pieces. Put 6 pineapple pieces between each pair of banana halves. Wrap a slice of ham firmly round each pair to hold the pieces together and secure with a wooden toothpick

❷ Cover the grid with metal foil. Grill the bananas for about 15 minutes, turning from time to time. Sprinkle with black pepper before serving.

Serves 4. Preparation time: about 10 minutes

4 bananas

3 slices pineapples

4 slices Parma or similar
   air-dried ham

freshly ground black pepper

Pineapple in grappa

This dish is quick and easy to prepare and makes a magnificent ending to a barbecue evening. If the Italian grappa is not available, any brandy can be used.

1 Peel and cut out the woody centre from the pineapple slices. Pour the grappa into a shallow dish. Put the pineapple slices in the grappa, turning them over several times. Cover and leave to stand for 20 minutes.

2 Cover the barbecue grid with foil. Melt the butter with the cream, cloves and confectioners' sugar in a small pan. Drain the pineapple slices, dip them in the butter and cream mixture and put them on the grid.

3 Grill the pineapple slices for about 5 minutes on each side until golden-brown. Arrange them plates and garnish with the raspberries. Sprinkle with confectioners' sugar and decorate with the mint leaves.

Serves 6. Preparation time: about 10 minutes + 20 minutes marinating

6 large slices pineapple

4–5 tablespoons grappa or brandy

8 tablespoons/4 oz/120 g butter

⅜ cup/3 fl oz/75 ml cream

1 teaspoon ground cloves

3 tablespoons confectioners' sugar

6 raspberries

12 leaves mint

1 pear

1 banana

1 mango

1 peach

3 tablespoons lemon juice

2 tablespoons liquid honey

2 tablespoons orange liqueur

3 oz/75 g crème fraîche

Hot fruit salad in foil

Barbecue desserts should be light and refreshing. This hot fruit salad is a perfect example: it is sweet with a refreshingly fruity taste, as well as being very low in calories.

❶ Peel the pear and banana. Remove the core from the pear and cut it into segments. Cut the banana into slices. Peel the mango and the peach and remove the pits (stones). Cut both fruits into segments.

❷ Stir the lemon juice, honey and liqueur into the fruit. Cut a piece of foil for each serving and divide the fruit salad among the pieces. Seal the parcels and grill for about 4 minutes. Check from time to time to see whether the fruit is cooked. The fruit should still have some bite.

❸ Remove from the barbecue. Open each parcel and garnish with a teaspoon of crème fraîche. Serve piping hot in the foil.

Serves 4. Preparation time: about 15 minutes

Grilled oranges

Large, juicy oranges are needed for this dessert. They are grilled wrapped in foil and eaten out of the skin.

❶ Cut the oranges in half and place each half on a piece of foil large enough to contain it. Stir together the confectioners' sugar, cloves and powderd cinnamon and sprinkle over the oranges.

❷ Dot a few flakes of butter on the oranges and gather the foil round the orange half but do not close the parcel completely. Cook on the barbecue for 3–5 minutes. Chop the filberts (hazelnuts) coarsely and sprinkle over the oranges. Serve immediately.

Serves 4. Preparation time: about 5 minutes

2 large untreated oranges

4 teaspoons confectioners' sugar

1 teaspoon ground cloves

1 teaspoon powderd cinnamon

4 tablespoons/2 oz/50 g butter

2 tablespoons filberts (hazelnuts)

Mangoes with rum

Grilled mangoes make a delicious dessert for a barbecue of Asian food. Here they are sprinkled with rum and served hot with cream. The mangoes used should be fairly firm, not overripe.

❶ Peel the mangoes. Remove the flesh from the stone with a sharp knife and cut into large pieces.

❷ Put the mango pieces on a plate, sprinkle with rum and leave to stand for about 5 minutes. Cover the grid with metal foil. Arrange the mango pieces on it and grill for about 4 minutes.

❸ Put the hot mango pieces on plates. Sprinkle with sugar, garnish with whipped cream and serve.

Serves 4. Preparation time: about 10 minutes + 5 minutes marinating

2 firm mangoes

4 tablespoons white rum

¼ cup/2 oz/50 g sugar

½ cup/4 fl oz/125 ml whipped cream

Guavas with lemon liqueur

Guavas are tropical fruit and very rich in vitamin C. Combined with candied fruit and flavored with lemon liqueur, they make a most sophisticated dessert.

1 Wash the guavas. Cut off and reserve the top with the stalk from each one. Using a spoon, remove the seeds and gently scoop out the flesh, leaving a little remaining on the sides.

2 Coarsely chop the flesh and put in a bowl. Finely chop the candied fruit and filberts (hazelnuts), using a sharp knife. Coat with a little flour and add these to the chopped guavas. Next add the lemon juice, lemon zest, lemon liqueur, and cinnamon. Mix together well.

3 Fill the hollowed-out guavas with this mixture. Put the lids back on top and wrap each fruit in a double layer of lightly oiled foil. Put the fruit parcels on the barbecue grill for 20–25 minutes. Arrange the guavas on plates and garnish each one with 2 fresh lychees.

Serves 4. Preparation time: about 10 minutes

4 guavas

1oz/30g mixed candied fruit

¾ oz/20 g filberts (hazelnuts)

juice and zest of 1 unpeeled lemon

1 tablespoon lemon liqueur

1 pinch powderd cinnamon

8 lychees

Tropical cocktail

A refreshing dessert made from tropical fruit that looks particularly attractive served in scooped-out oranges. Carambola is a tropical fruit sometimes known as star fruit, because of its shape.

3 large untreated pomelos

1 carambola

1 banana

1 tablespoon lemon juice

½ fresh pineapple

1 mango

1 papaya

4 tablespoons maple syrup

2 tablespoons coconut milk

2 tablespoons grated coconut

❶ Cut the pomelos in half, scoop out the flesh with a spoon and cut into bite-sized pieces. Cut the carambola into thin slices. Peel the bananas, cut into slices and sprinkle with lemon juice.

❷ Remove the pineapple skin with a sharp knife, cut out the stalk and cut the flesh into small pieces. Peel the mango, loosen the flesh from the pit (stone) with a sharp knife and cut into strips. Cut the papaya in half, peel, remove the seeds and cut the flesh into cubes.

❸ Put all the fruit in a bowl. Heat the maple syrup and coconut milk and pour gently over the fruit. Spoon this fruit mixture into the hollowed-out pomelos. Wrap each half-pomelo in foil and grill for about 8 minutes over medium heat. Take the pomelos out of the foil, arrange on plates and sprinkle the hot fruit with grated coconut.

Serves 6. Preparation time: about 30 minutes

Fruit kebabs with raspberry coulis

Any seasonal fruit can be used for this dessert so it can be varied to taste. They are flavored with cinnamon and cardamom and the final delicious touch is the hot raspberry coulis.

1 apple

1 teaspoon lemon juice

2 nectarines

2 oranges

12 strawberries

½ cup/4 fl oz/125 ml rum

¼ cup/2 oz/60 g sugar

1 teaspoon powderd cinnamon

1 pinch ground cardamom

9 oz/250 g raspberries

3 tablespoons confectioners' sugar

❶ Peel and core the apple. Cut into slices and sprinkle with lemon juice. Cut the nectarines in half, remove the pit (stone) and cut into slices. Peel the oranges, remove the pith and cut into slices ¾ in/2 cm thick. Remove the stalk from the strawberries.

❷ Sprinkle the rum on the fruit and mix together the sugar, cinnamon and cardamom in a large, shallow dish. Dip the slices of fruit and strawberries into the mixture and thread them on a skewer in a colorful sequence. Line the grid with foil and grill for about 10–15 minutes until the sugar turns brown, turning the skewers several times.

❸ Meanwhile, heat the raspberries with the confectioners' sugar in a small saucepan and simmer for 2 minutes. Pour this hot sauce over the fruit kebabs.

Serves 4–6. Preparation time: about 20 minutes

Barbecued apple and pear segments

Similar to a fruit salad, this simple dessert requires very little preparation. Sweet apples and firm pears are needed for this recipe.

1 Peel the apples and pears, cut them in half and remove the cores. Cut the fruit into segments.

2 Mix together the lemon juice and cider and pour over the fruit. Dot flakes of butter on an aluminum foil tray, arrange the fruit segments on top and grill over medium for about 5-8 minutes.

3 Put the hot fruit segments in a large bowl and stir in the orange jello (jelly). Sprinkle with sugar to taste.

Serves 4. Preparation time: about 15 minutes

2 apples

2 pears

1 tablespoon lemon juice

3 tablespoons cider

2 tablespoons/1 oz/30 g butter

3½ oz/100 g orange jello (jelly)

sugar to taste

Baked apple

Baked apple is not just a delicious winter dish. It can be prepared on the barbecue in summer and served as a dessert. In this recipe the apples are filled with pieces of pineapple and mandarin oranges.

1 Wash the apples, remove the cores and immediately sprinkle the inside with lemon juice.

2 Slice the pineapples into small pieces, peel the mandarin oranges and separate into pieces. Cut each piece in half with a knife. Put the pieces of fruit into a pan. Add the raisins, cardamom, sugar, butter and coconut milk. Cook together for about 5 minutes, until half the liquid has evaporated.

3 Put each apple on a double layer of foil. Fill the core with the fruit mixture. Wrap the foil tightly round each apple. Cook over medium heat at the edge of the barbecue for about 45 minutes, turning occasionally. Remove the apples from the foil and serve with whipped cream.

Serves 4. Preparation time: about 15 minutes

4 apples

1 tablespoon lemon juice

2 slices pineapple

2 mandarin oranges

1 tablespoons raisins

1 pinch cardamom

¼ cup/2 oz/60 g brown sugar

2 tablespoons/1 oz/30 g butter

2 tablespoons coconut milk

3½ oz/100 g whipped cream

Fruit kebab

Kebabs need not always be savory – they can also be sweet and make delicious desserts. Any kind of fruit can be used as long as the flesh is firm enough to thread on a skewer.

2 apples

2 firm pears

1 tablespoon lemon juice

2 firm nectarines

2 firm figs

9 oz/250 g strawberries

6 tablespoons/3 oz/75 g butter

⅜ cup/3 oz/75 g confectioners' sugar

1 packet vanilla sugar

1 tablespoon Cointreau

juice and zest of 1 orange

❶ Wash the apples and the pears, cut into quarters and remove the cores. Cut the segments in half diagonally and sprinkle with lemon juice.

❷ Wash the nectarines, remove the pits (stones) and cut into eight segments. Cut the figs into quarters. Wash the strawberries, pat dry and cut the strawberries in half. Thread the pieces of fruit on 6 skewers, using each kind in turn.

❸ Melt the butter in a small saucepan. Stir in the confectioners' sugar and the vanilla sugar. Add the Cointreau, orange juice and orange zest. Brush the mixture on the fruit kebabs and barbecue over medium heat for 5 minutes. Serve hot.

Serves 6. Preparation time:

Marinades, Sauces & Dips

Creamed horseradish

This tasty relish is quick and easy to make. The sharp flavor of the horseradish is counterbalanced by the mildness of the cream and is therefore quite digestible. Creamed horseradish can be served with most fish and it is also excellent with meat, particularly beef, and sausages.

7 oz/200 g whipping cream

1 tablespoon horseradish (fresh or preserved)

salt

sugar

1 teaspoon lemon juice

❶ Beat the cream in a bowl until stiff.

❷ Peel the horseradish and grate finely.

❸ Fold the horseradish into the cream. Season to taste with salt, sugar, and lemon juice.

Serves 4. Preparation time: about 10 minutes

Lime-flavored hollandaise sauce

Limes have a much more intense flavour than lemons, so it is well worth trying to find them for this sauce.

4 egg yolks

2 teaspoons lemon juice

salt

freshly ground white pepper

1½ cups/9 oz/250 g butter, melted

1 untreated lime

freshly ground pepper

❶ Mix the lemon juice, salt and pepper with the egg yolks and whisk vigorously to obtain a creamy texture. Put in a bowl set above a pan of water brought to the boil. Keep the water simmering and stir continuously until the sauce thickens. Add the warm melted butter little by little, whisking all the time.

❷ Wash the lime under running hot water, wipe dry and grate 1–2 teaspoons of zest. Stir the zest into the hollandaise and season with pepper.

Serves 4. Preparation time: about 15 minutes

Classic mayonnaise

Home-made mayonnaise tastes much better than what can be bought in a jar, and it is quite quick to make. It is important that all the ingredients should be at room temperature or the mayonnaise may curdle. It is a perfect accompaniment to fish and vegetables.

❶ Put the egg yolks with the salt, sugar, pepper, mustard and lemon juice in a bowl and whisk together to obtain a creamy mixture.

❷ Add the oil drop by drop to start with, whisking continuously. Do not be too impatient or the mayonnaise will separate. (If it does, put a new egg yolk in a clean bowl and slowly whisk in the separated mixture.)

❸ As the sauce begins to thicken the oil can be added a little more quickly. Continue until the mayonnaise has the consistency of a thick creamy sauce.

❹ If the mayonnaise is too thick it can be thinned it with lemon juice or vinegar. If it is not thick enough, whisk in more oil.

Serves 4–6. Preparation time: about 20 minutes

2 egg yolks

salt

sugar

freshly ground white pepper

1 teaspoon mustard

1–2 teaspoons lemon juice or vinegar

1¼ cups/10 fl oz/300 ml olive oil

Tomato mayonnaise

Since it uses prepared mayonnaise, this is easier to make than a traditional mayonnaise and is therefore a welcome alternative. It is delicious served as a dip with raw vegetables such as carrots or celery.

❶ Peel the scallions (spring onions) and cut into thin rings

❷ Heat the olive oil in a saucepan, add the onions and fry gently. Next stir in the tomato puree.

❸ Leave to cool in a bowl, then stir in the mayonnaise.

❹ Season with Tabasco, salt, sugar and pepper.

Serves 4. Preparation time: about 20 minutes

2 scallions (spring onions)

2 tablespoons olive oil

3 tablespoons tomato paste

5 oz/150 g mayonnaise (or mayonnaise light)

Tabasco

salt

sugar

freshly ground white pepper

7 oz/200 g mixed (green and
black) pitted olives

4 medium cloves garlic

4 sprigs thyme

2 tablespoons tarragon mustard

½ cup/3½ fl oz/100 ml olive oil

juice of 1 lemon

salt

freshly ground pepper

Olive sauce

The slightly bitter, sharp taste of the olives give this sauce a very distinctive taste. It is an ideal accompaniment for sea fish, shellfish and lamb-based dishes. It is also excellent as a starter, spread on bread.

❶ Chop the olives and cloves of garlic finely or puree in the blender.

❷ Wash the thyme, pat dry, chop finely, and stir in the tarragon mustard.

❸ Add the olive oil little by little. Stir in the chopped olives and garlic to obtain a smooth paste.

❹ Season to taste with lemon juice, salt and pepper.

Serves 8–10. Preparation time: about 15 minutes

3½ oz/100 g white bread

½ cup/4 fl oz/125 ml vegetable
  broth (stock)

1 egg yolk

2–4 cloves garlic

½ cup/4 fl oz/125 ml olive oil

salt

pepper

1 tablespoon oregano

6 tablespoons fresh herbs

2 small shallots

2 cloves garlic

1 cup/8 fl oz/250 ml yogurt

2 tablespoons olive oil

2 tablespoons balsamic vinegar

freshly ground pepper

salt

Garlic sauce

Garlic sauce can be served with any grilled food, whether fish, meat or vegetables. It is also delicious spread on toast, but it is best to avoid it the day before an important appointment!

❶ Cut white bread into slices, remove the crusts and soak in the vegetable stock.

❷ Puree the bread with the egg yolk, salt and pepper in a blender.

❸ Peel the cloves of garlic and chop coarsely. Keeping the blender running, add it to the sauce, then gradually add the olive oil.

❹ Finally add the oregano.

Serves 6. Preparation time: about 15 minutes

Yogurt and herb sauce

The garlic can easily be omitted from this deliciously refreshing sauce if you prefer it without.

❶ Wash the herbs, pat dry and chop finely. Peel the shallots and chop finely.

❷ Peel and crush or press the garlic. Mix well and stir into a smooth sauce together with the other ingredients.

Serves 4. Preparation time: about 10 minutes

Barbecue sauce

As the name suggests this is the traditional spicy barbecue sauce, delicious served with any kind of meat. In particular it is an indispensable accompaniment to barbecued chicken wings.

❶ Put mustard, wine, honey, soy sauce, oil and catsup in a pan and stir well.

❷ Simmer for about 5 minutes.

❸ Season with salt, pepper, and Tabasco or chili oil.

Serves 4. Preparation time: about 10 minutes

**5 tablespoons strong mustard
  (or best Dijon mustard)**

5 tablespoons dry white wine

**5 tablespoons mild honey
  (such as lime honey)**

3 tablespoons soy sauce

2 tablespoons sunflower oil

**5 tablespoons catsup (tomato
  ketchup)**

salt

black pepper

Tabasco or chili oil to taste

English mint sauce

There are over 20 different kinds of mint with variations in taste, but they all share one component, menthol. This gives mint its distinctive refreshing flavor. The sugar is important because it helps the mint to develop its full aroma. Mint sauce is a favorite with lamb.

❶ Dissolve the sugar in 2 tablespoons of boiling. Wash the mint leaves and chop them very finely. Put them in a small bowl and add dissolved sugar.

❷ Leave to cool, then add the vinegar.

❸ Stand for a few hours before serving.

Serves 6. Preparation time: about 15 minutes + standing time

**5 tablespoons finely chopped
  fresh mint**

5 tablespoons white wine vinegar

2 teaspoons sugar

Herb sauce

1 teaspoon mustard

½ cup/4 fl oz/125 ml low fat
   yogurt

1 tablespoon lemon juice

salt

freshly ground pepper

2 tablespoons chopped herbs:
   parsley, chives, chervil, dill,
   cilantro (green coriander)

½ cup/3½ fl oz /100 ml whipping
   cream

The herbs used to flavor this sauce can be varied according to taste or
depending on what herbs are available.

1 Stir the mustard, yogurt and lemon juice together to make a smooth sauce.
Season with salt and pepper and add the herbs.

2 Whip the cream until thick and stir into the herb sauce.

Serves 4. Preparation time: about 5 minutes

Tarragon sauce

2 eggs

juice of 1 lemon

1½ cups/12 fl oz/375 ml cream

4 teaspoons medium strong
   mustard

4 tablespoons tarragon vinegar

2 bunches tarragon

olive oil

salt

freshly ground pepper

The appearance and taste of this sauce can be altered by adding 2–3
peeled, chopped tomatoes to it.

Stir the eggs, lemon, cream, mustard and tarragon vinegar together. Add the
finely chopped tarragon and olive oil. Season with salt and pepper.

Serves 4. Preparation time: about 5 minutes

3 tablespoons parsley

1 tablespoon chopped chives

1 tablespoon basil

1 teaspoon lovage

1 teaspoon thyme

1 teaspoon oregano

1 cup/8 oz/225 g butter

2 cloves garlic

salt

pepper

2 teaspoons lemon juice

Herb butter

Herb butter is very popular and delicious served with meat and potatoes. It is also excellent with fish. The herbs given in the recipe are only a suggestion and can be varied according to taste, but they must be fresh, not dried.

❶ Take the butter out of the refrigerator and leave to soften at room temperature.

❷ Wash and chop the parsley, chives, basil and lovage, then mix them together. Add the thyme and oregano. Put 3 tablespoons of this herb mixture to one side.

❸ Stir the rest of the herb mixture and the lemon juice into the softened butter. Peel the cloves of garlic, put through a garlic press and add to the butter mixture. Season with salt and pepper.

❹ Shape the butter mixture into a roll in foil or waxed (greaseproof) paper.

❺ Sprinkle the reserved herbs on a piece of foil. Roll the shaped butter over these herbs, pressing slightly, so that the butter is covered with them.

❻ Wrap in foil and cool in the refrigerator

Serves 4. Preparation time: about 15 minutes

9 oz/250 g skimmed milk low-fat
   soft cheese (quark)

2 tablespoons natural yogurt

1 red bell (sweet) pepper

1 tomato

salt

pepper

1 tablespoon prepared paprika
   paste (ajwar)

Paprika dip

This dip is refreshing, light and almost calorie-free. It is quick and easy to prepare and is therefore ideal for barbecues. It is also very good served with bread and raw vegetable crudités as an appetizer.

❶ Wash the peppers and tomatoes, then remove the seeds. Dice both finely.

❷ Mix together the low-fat soft cheese (quark) and yogurt.

❸ Stir in the diced vegetables.

❹ Season with salt, pepper and a little ajwar.

Serves 6–8. Preparation time: about 10 minutes

Tomato and basil sauce

This tomato and basil sauce can be served hot or cold with asparagus. It is excellent accompanied by crusty French bread.

❶ Wash the tomatoes and cut in half. Chop the flesh finely. Wash the basil, pat dry and cut the leaves into thin strips.

❷ Peel the shallots, dice finely and fry them in butter. Stir in the vinegar, oil, white wine and lemon juice. Bring to the boil and reduce the liquid to two-thirds.

❸ Stir the tomatoes and basil into the sauce and season with salt and pepper.

Serves 4. Preparation time: about 30 minutes

6 tomatoes

2 bunch basil

3 shallots

1 tablespoon/½ oz/15 g butter

6 teaspoons white wine vinegar

4 tablespoons/2 fl oz/60 ml oil

1½ cups/12 fl oz/375 ml white
   wine

3 tablespoons lemon juice

salt

freshly ground pepper

Apple and horseradish dip

Fresh horseradish has an extremely strong aroma that can make the eyes water, as when peeling onions. Be very careful not to get any in the eye when grating it. In this recipe the apples soften the strength of the horseradish, but it remains a very piquant dip.

1 Peel the apples, remove the cores and cut in half. Cut each half-apple into quarters and put in a pan.

2 Add the vegetable stock, cider, lemon juice and sugar. Cook all together until the apples have softened. Puree the soft apple in a blender or food processor.

3 Peel the horseradish and grate finely.

4 Stir the grated horseradish into the crème fraîche. Add the apple puree and mix together well. Season to taste with salt.

Serves 6–8. Preparation time: about 25 minutes

2 apples
2 tablespoons lemon juice
½ cup/4 fl oz/125 ml cider
1 tablespoon sugar
3½ oz/100 g horseradish
7 oz/200 g crème fraîche
salt

Herb dip

The herb dip can be varied endlessly, because it always tastes good whatever combination and proportion of herbs is used. Chives, parsley, basil, dill and cress are readily available in all seasons.

1 Wash the herbs, shake them dry and chop the leaves finely. Peel the onion and chop finely. Toast the pine kernels in a pan without fat, then chop them very finely.

2 Stir together the pine kernels, cheese, yogurt, and herb-onion mixture. Season the dip generously with salt and pepper.

Serves 6–8. Preparation time: about 10 minutes

1 bunch fresh assorted herbs
1 small onion
1 tablespoon pine kernels
9 oz/250 g soft cheese
2 tablespoons yogurt
salt
freshly ground black pepper

1½ lb/700 g ripe tomatoes

2 scallions (spring onions)

2 cloves garlic

½ bunch cilentro (green coriander) or parsley

1 small red chili pod

4 tablespoons olive oil

salt

1 teaspoon sugar

some Tabasco to taste

Spicy tomato sauce

This sauce is tasty alternative for lovers of spicy, exotic foods. The cilentro (green coriander) gives the sauce a very distinctive flavor. A non-Oriental version can be made by using parsley instead of cilentro.

❶ Cut a cross in the stalk end of the tomatoes with a sharp knife. Pour boiling water over them and peel.

❷ Cut the tomatoes in half, remove the seeds with a teaspoon and dice very finely. Strain the tomato juice through a sieve to separate from the seeds.

❸ Add a little of the tomato juice to the tomato flesh to thin the sauce a little.

❹ Peel and finely chop the scallions (spring onions) and cloves of garlic. Wash the cilentro or parsley and chop finely. Wash the chili, remove the seeds and cut into very small pieces. Wash the hands after handling the chili!

❺ Add all the ingredients together with the olive oil to the tomatoes and stir well. Season to taste with salt, sugar and tabasco.

Serves 4. Preparation time: about 20 minutes

Garlic herb marinade for lamb

When meat is marinated overnight it acquires a particular aroma and intensity of flavor. This marinade is especially good for grilled lamb cutlets. It can also be used to enhance the taste of a roasted shoulder or leg of lamb.

For 4 lamb cutlets:

4 cloves garlic

2 tablespoons red wine

2 tablespoons chopped fresh herbs (to choice)

8 tablespoons olive oil

4 lamb cutlets

salt

freshly ground black pepper

❶ Peel the cloves of garlic and push through a garlic press.

❷ Heat the red wine, pour in the olive oil, add the chopped herbs and garlic paste and mix well to incorporate all the ingredients.

❸ Coat the lamb cutlets generously on both sides with the marinade and leave to stand for at least 2 hours, but preferably overnight.

❹ Remove the meat from the marinade, pat dry with paper towels and grill for about 5 minutes on both sides. Season with salt and pepper.

Serves 4. Preparation time: about 10 minutes + 1–2 hours marinating

Ginger marinade for chicken

Ginger was used as a meat seasoning throughout Europe in the Middle Ages, but during the 18th century this spice largely vanished from the European scene. Today, it is best known as a seasoning used in Chinese cuisine. Since ground ginger loses its aroma quickly, it is best to use fresh ginger and grate it when required.

For 4 chicken thighs:

2 tablespoons soy-sauce

2 tablespoons white wine-vinegar

4 tablespoons peanut (ground nut) oil

1 tablespoons freshly grated or ground ginger

1 pinch chili powder

2 tablespoons honey

❶ Mix the soy sauce, vinegar, peanut oil and ginger. Season with the chili powder.

❷ Spread the marinade thickly over chicken thighs on all sides. Cover and leave to stand for at least 1–2 hours, or overnight if possible. Just before grilling the chicken thighs, spread the honey over them. This adds a pleasant sweetness.

Preparation time: about 5 minutes

Lemon marinade for fish

A classic fish marinade that gives fish a very special aroma. For barbecuing, a firm-fleshed fish with few bones is perfect, such as tuna or swordfish. The marinade can also be served as a sauce, for instance with shellfish.

❶ Mix together the lemon juice, pepper, mustard and 4 tablespoon of olive oil.

❷ Peel the onion, chop very finely and add to the mixture. Season with salt and pepper.

❸ Brush the fish steaks on both sides with this marinade and let stand for at least 2 hours or overnight.

❹ Remove the fish fillets from the marinade, wipe dry with paper towels and grill on foil for 10–15 minutes on both sides.

Serves 4. Preparation time: about 10 minutes + 2 hours marinating

juice of 1 lemon

1 teaspoon pepper

2 teaspoons Dijon mustard

6 tablespoons olive oil

1 onion

herb salt

freshly ground mixed colored pepper

4 steaks firm fish, such as swordfish

Side Dishes

18 oz/500 g all-purpose (plain) flour

1¼ cups/10 fl oz/300 ml lukewarm water

1 teaspoon dried yeast

1 teaspoon sugar

1½ tablespoons/¾ oz/20 g soft margarine or butter

3½ oz/100 g baking soda (bicarbonate of soda)

3 tablespoons coarse ground salt

Home-made pretzels

Home-made bread is always a treat. But few people make their own pretzels, partly because of poaching process that precedes baking. But this is in fact quite an easy procedure. Baking soda (bicarbonate of soda) is available from supermarkets or pharmacies.

❶ Dissolve the yeast with the sugar in the lukewarm water. Wait until the yeast starts to produce bubbles.

❷ Sieve the flour into a bowl, make a hollow in the middle and pour the dissolved yeast mixture into it.

❸ Add the margarine or butter. Knead to a smooth dough. Stand in a warm place for about 30 minutes. Roll the dough into cylindrical lengths and shape the pretzels (see photograph). Leave them to stand again.

❹ Meanwhile bring 4½ cups/1¾ pints/1 litre of water with baking soda to the boil. Carefully dip the pretzels into the boiling water using a ladle and wait till they rise to the surface. Then take them out and drain.

❺ Sprinkle the pretzels with salt, put on a greased baking-sheet and bake on the middle shelf in the oven at 425°F (220°C), Gas mark 7 for 10–15 minutes, or until golden brown. Leave to cool on a grid.

Serves 4. Preparation time: about 25 minutes + standing time

Bacon and cabbage salad

This is a perfect recipe for those who like a nourishing salad. It is usually served with meat such as roast pork or pork spareribs. It is easy to make but fairly time-consuming, so begin the preparations 2 or 3 hours before the meal.

1 head white cabbage

1 cup/8 fl oz/250 ml vegetable broth (stock)

10 tablespoons herb vinegar

1 teaspoon caraway seeds

9 oz/250 g diced bacon

salt

freshly ground black pepper

❶ Cut the white cabbage in half. Remove the stalky end and cut into thin strips. Then blanch briefly in slightly salted boiling water, remove, and drain. Put in a salad bowl while still hot.

❷ Bring the vegetable broth (stock) to the boil with the vinegar and caraway seeds. Pour over the cabbage and stir.

❸ Fry the diced bacon in a pan until crisp and stir into the salad. Season with salt and pepper.

❹ Cover the bowl and leave the salad to stand for 1–2 hours.

Serves 6. Preparation time: about 25 minutes + 2 hours standing time

Tomato salad

Tomato salad is undoubtedly one of the most traditional salads, and there are countless recipes for it. Naturally, the flavor of the tomatoes is all-important in this case, so tomatoes grown out of doors are preferable to greenhouse tomatoes. The herbs should be fresh, so if basil is not available, use cress, dill, chives or parsley instead.

❶ Remove the stalks of the tomatoes, wash, dry and cut each into eight pieces.

❷ Peel the onions and chop finely or cut into rings.

❸ Pluck the basil leaves from the stalks and chop finely.

❹ Peel the cloves of garlic and push through the garlic press. Then stir in the vinegar, salt, sugar and mustard. Pour in the olive oil little by little and season with pepper.

❺ Put the tomatoes, onions and basil in a bowl. Pour the dressing over the salad and stir gently. Sprinkle with freshly ground pepper.

Serves 4–6. Preparation time: about 10 minutes

2¼ lb/1 kg tomatoes
1 medium red onion
1 bunch fresh basil or other herbs
1 clove garlic
1 teaspoon salt
2 teaspoons sugar
2 teaspoons strong mustard
4 tablespoons balsamic vinegar
8 tablespoons olive oil
freshly ground black pepper

Barbecued flat bread

This flat bread recipe is perfect for barbecues away from home because it can be rolled round sausages, salad and dips, making plates and cutlery unnecessary. The dough can be quickly and easily prepared in advance at home and then taken to where it is to be used.

❶ Sift the flour and mix in the salt. Stir in ¾ cup/6 fl oz/175 ml of warm water and knead to make a smooth dough without lumps.

❷ Dust the dough with flour and cover. Leave in a warm place for 20 minutes.

❸ Dust the hands with flour and divide the dough into 8 pieces. Roll out each one into a thin round.

❹ To cook, brush the pieces with olive oil and sprinkle with oregano. Cover the grid with metal foil. Grill the bread for 2–3 minutes on each side.

Serves 4. Preparation time: about 10 minutes + 20 minutes resting time

2½ cups/9 oz/250 g all-purpose (plain) flour
¾ cup/6 fl oz/175 ml warm water
1 teaspoon salt
flour
3 tablespoons olive oil
2 teaspoons oregano

1 small head Iceberg lettuce

1 head radicchio

1 pack oak leaf or lamb's lettuce

1 cucumber

2–4 tomatoes

1 bunch scallions (spring onions)

1 bunch chives

4 tablespoons sherry vinegar

4 tablespoons sherry

8 tablespoons olive oil

salt

freshly ground white pepper

1–2 large cucumbers

14 oz/400 g sheep's milk cheese (feta)

1 bunch fresh mint or dill

4 tablespoons herb vinegar

salt

freshly ground black pepper

8 tablespoons olive oil

Summer salad

Mixed salad is one of the classic dishes for a barbecue evening. The sherry dressing used in this recipe is what makes all the difference. Pour it onto the salad at the last minute. The salad leaves used can be varied depending to what is available.

❶ Wash the salad leaves carefully. Pat dry and tear into bite-size pieces.

❷ Wash the cucumber and tomatoes and cut into thin slices. Cut the scallions (spring onions) into rings and stir all the ingredients together in a large bowl. Chop the chives finely and put to one side.

❸ Stir the sherry and vinegar together and season with salt and pepper. Add the olive oil little by little.

❹ Pour the dressing over the salad and stir well. Sprinkle the chives on top.

Serves 4. Preparation time: about 15 minutes

Cucumber salad with sheep's milk cheese

This recipe is particularly pleasant on hot summer days. The freshness of the cucumber combined with the acid of the sheep's milk cheese is a joy to the palate. The salad goes well with sausages or grilled meat.

❶ Peel the cucumbers and slice thinly into a salad bowl. Cut the cheese into small dice or crumble with the fingers directly into the salad.

❷ Wash the mint or dill and shake dry. Finely chop the leaves and sprinkle over the salad.

❸ Mix the vinegar with salt and pepper. Mix in the olive oil. Pour the dressing over the salad and mix carefully.

Serves 4. Preparation time: about 10 minutes

9 oz/250 g small pickled gherkins

3 tablespoons/1½ oz/40 g salt

½ small head cauliflower

4½ oz/125 g carrots

4½ oz/125 g small corn cobs

1 red bell (sweet) pepper

3½ oz/100 g cocktail onions

2¼ cups/17 fl oz/500 ml red wine vinegar

¼ cup/2 oz/50 g sugar

2 bay leaves

5 allspice

freshly ground black pepper

2 teaspoons mustard seeds

Home-made mixed pickles

These pickles take some time to prepare but the result is worth it, since home-made pickles are even nicer than bought ones. Stored in a cool, dark place, they will keep for up to six months.

❶ The night before, carefully wash the gherkins and leave them to soak for 12 hours in 2¼ cups/17 fl oz/500 ml of salted water.

❷ Wash the vegetables and peel if necessary. Separate the cauliflower into florets, cut the carrots into slices and the pepper into strips.

❸ Blanch these vegetables in boiling water for 5 minutes. Remove and immerse briefly in very cold water.

❹ Peel the onions. Remove the gherkins from the salted water and rinse.

❺ Bring the vinegar to the boil with 1½ cups/12 fl oz/375 ml water and ¼ cup/2 oz/50 g sugar. Put the vegetables with the bay leaves, pepper, allspice, and mustard seeds in a preserving jar. Fill the jar with the liquid.

❻ After 3–4 days, drain the liquid from the preserving jar and bring it to the boil again. Then pour it back over the pickles.

Serves 6–8. Preparation time: about 40 minutes + 4 days standing time

Potato salad

This delicious potato salad should be left to stand for at least half-an-hour before serving so that its flavor will develop to the full. The onions add a piquant touch to the salad, while the gherkins and parsley add a refreshing note. The parsley may be replaced by chives or cress.

2¼ lb/1 kg waxy potatoes

1 gherkin

2 onions

1 cup/8 fl oz/250 ml vegetable broth (stock)

5 tablespoons herb vinegar

salt

1 pinch sugar

1 tablespoon sharp or Dijon mustard

4 tablespoons corn oil

freshly ground black pepper

1 bunch parsley

❶ Wash the potatoes well and boil for about 20 minutes. Peel while still hot and cut into thin slices.

❷ Peel the gherkins, cut into strips or slices and stir into the potatoes.

❸ Peel the onions and chop finely.

❹ Bring the vegetable broth (stock), vinegar, salt, sugar, and onions to the boil and stir in the mustard and oil. Pour the dressing over the salad. Season with salt and pepper.

❺ Wash the parsley, pat dry with paper towels, divide into small sprigs and sprinkle over the salad.

❺ Cover and leave to stand for at least 30 minutes. Stir again before serving.

Serves 4. Preparation time: about 50 minutes + 30 minutes standing time

Bell (sweet) peppers in olive oil

Peppers in olive oil are very popular and look very appetizing. Available in delicatessens, they are also easy to make at home and delicious served with white bread, cheese and olives, as well as barbecued dishes.

1 Wash the peppers and pat dry. Put them on a baking sheet and roast in the oven at 350°F (180°C), Gas mark 4 until they begin to blister, turning them from time to time.

2 Then wrap the peppers in a cool, damp cloth and leave for 5 minutes. Rub off the black skin and peel off the rest of the skin. Finally, remove the stalk.

3 Put the vinegar, water, salt and pepper in a large bowl and stir until the salt has dissolved. Then add the peppers. Cover and leave to stand for 2–3 hours.

4 Peel the cloves of garlic and slice thinly. Remove the peppers from the marinade and put on a plate. Mix the garlic and olive oil together and pour over the peppers.

5 Cover with foil and refrigerate overnight.

Serves 4. Preparation time: about 30 minutes + 12 hours standing time

4 large red or yellow bell (sweet) peppers

½ cup/4 fl oz/125 ml balsamic vinegar

½ cup/4 fl oz/125 ml water

1 tablespoon salt

freshly ground black pepper

4 cloves garlic

⅞ cup/7 fl oz/200 ml olive oil

Index

Alphabetical list of recipes

List of recipes by category

Concept and execution:
twinbooks, Munich
Editorial: twinbooks, Munich
(Gisela Witt, Madeleine Willing,
Petra Neumayer, Dagmar Fronius-
Gaier, Julia Nunes, Simone Steger,
Sonya Mayer)
Layout and typesetting: twinbooks,
Munich (Hubert Medien Design,
Munich)
English translation and typesetting:
Rosetta International, London
Photography: twinbooks, Munich
(Christian Kargl, Brigitte Sporrer,
Alena Hrbkova)
Food styling: twinbooks, Munich
(Tim Landsberg)
© cover photograph: StockFood
Munich/Picture Box, Ouddeken
Printing and binding: Druckerei
Appl, Wemding

© 2002 DuMont monte Verlag, Köln
(DuMont monte UK, London)

ISBN 3-8320-7095-8

Printed in Germany

The recipes in this book have been
carefully researched and tested.
However, neither the author nor
the publishers can be held liable
for the contents of this book.

Acknowledgements:
The editor and publisher thank the
following for their help in creating
this book:
Weber Stephen Deutschland
GmbH, Ellerbek
Ketchum GmbH, Munich

Picture Credits:
All photographs by Christian Kargl
with the exception of pp 20, 21, 29,
33, 36, 37, 42, 44, 46, 47, 48, 49, 51,
54, 57, 58, 60, 62, 66, 70, 71, 74, 75,
77, 78, 82, 84, 85, 88, 89, 92, 93, 96,
103, 107, 110, 116b, 120, 122, 124,
128, 132, 133, 139, 143, 144, 150,
153, 154, 158 (Brigitte
Sporrer/Alena Hrbkova), 11, 15
(Weber Stephen Deutschland
GmbH), 10 (Ketchum GmbH)

The author:
Elisabeth Lang is trained cook. She
has worked in various hotels and
restaurants in and around her home
town of Weilheim in Bavaria. For
several years she has also devoted
herself to her other main interest,
writing. As a freelance writer she has
regularly contributed articles to
magazines. This is her first book.

Photographers:
Christian Kargl acquired his
interest in cooking from working
as assistant to a food
photographer. He works mainly in
his own studio in Munich.

Brigitte Sporrer and Alena
Hrbkova met each other while
training as photographers in
Munich, Germany. After working
as assistants to various advertising
and food photographers, they now
each have their own studios in
Munich and Prague respectively.

Food stylist:
Tim Landsberg, trained cook from
Bonn, works in Munich as a
freelance food stylist for clients
including print and television
advertising companies. He also
works on cookery books.